IN OLD PHOTO

C000182005

AROUND
CRYSTAL PALACE
& PENGE

DAVID R. JOHNSON

SUTTON PUBLISHING

Sutton Publishing Limited
Phoenix Mill · Thrupp · Stroud
Gloucestershire · GL5 2BU

First published 2004

Title page photograph: Joseph Paxton epitomised the confident Victorian age. He is shown here with part of his best-known creation, the Crystal Palace. *(Illustrated London News)*

British Library Cataloguing in Publication Data
A catalogue record for this book is available from the British Library.

ISBN 0-7509-3124-8

Typeset in 10.5/13.5 Photina.
Typesetting and origination by
Sutton Publishing Limited.
Printed and bound in England by
J.H. Haynes & Co. Ltd, Sparkford.

Nancy Tonkin and my brother, Leonard Johnson, started to write a book on the Crystal Palace some ten years ago. Eventually Nancy died and my brother suffered from bad health, so I was asked to continue the work. The book is dedicated to these two considerable local historians.

CONTENTS

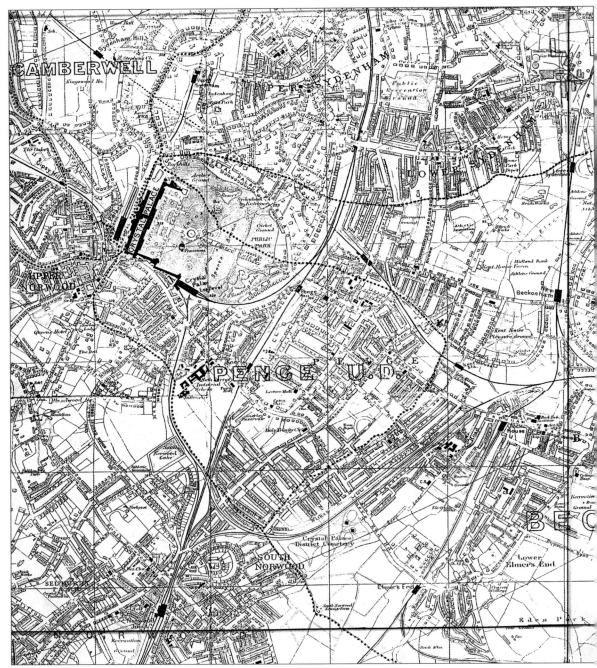

The 1910 boundaries are marked with dots on this map, which shows the four districts that met at the Vicar's Oak, which originally stood at the southern end of Crystal Palace Parade. Two more districts are at the northern end of the Parade; Sydenham, part of Lewisham, met the 'finger of land' which was part of Beckenham. Following on clockwise are Penge, Croydon, Lambeth and Dulwich, part of Camberwell. With Penge and Beckenham as part of Bromley the number of districts meeting near the Crystal Palace was reduced in 1965 from six to five. The border along Crystal Palace Parade has been changed so that Southwark, which includes Dulwich and the old Camberwell, no longer stretches across the road into what was the site of the Palace. The whole of the Crystal Palace Park is now in the London Borough of Bromley.

FOREWORD

The Crystal Palace in London's southern suburbs was opened on 10 June 1854 by Queen Victoria, who thought the building beautiful. This book's publication in 2004 coincides with the 150th anniversary of that significant event. Local people and events, whether they have direct Crystal Palace connections or not, are also examined. The Great Exhibition of 1851 had been such a success, helped largely by the building itself, that it was resurrected in the grounds of Penge Place. Already, before the existence of the Crystal Palace, developers had taken an interest in what was considered a healthy and attractive area. The railway was already providing commuters with a service. The journey to town took about the same time as in the early twenty-first century. The arrival of the Palace speeded house building in the vicinity and influenced the character of the Crystal Palace district. The present generation's environment was shaped by mid-nineteenth-century decisions. One example is the Crystal Palace Park, which otherwise would have been 'developed' by now.

Paxton was mainly responsible for creating the grounds; with hindsight, he and his colleagues made over-lavish expenditure on the 1854 elaborate Palace and gardens. The remains of the Italian gardens bear witness to what was the created backdrop, so important to 'a blazing arch of lucid glass' as William Thackeray, the novelist, described the building on the hill. Thackeray had local interests especially with Kent House Farm, not a mile from the Palace gates.

Newspapers, indirectly or directly reported, give a flavour of national and local events over the last 150 years. Not in strict chronological order they include, from the *Beckenham Journal*, June 1878:

Trespassing. Before the Bromley Bench on Monday . . . the following boys were charged with trespassing on fields belonging to Mr Langlands of Kent House Farm, and damaging grass to the value of 6d.; viz: Joseph Weedon, Croydon Villas, Croydon Road, W. Otaway . . . Clark . . . Atkins . . . Whitehead . . . Bacon . . . Veazey . . . Hall . . . Knell . . . Dears . . . and W.H. Linfoot, Pawleyne Arms . . . all in Penge. P.C.s 106 and 108 gave evidence as to their having seen the lads bathing in the Pool river on the afternoon of Sunday, 12th May, on the property of the prosecutor. Dears was fined 11s. 2d., Knell 13s. 8d, and the others 10s. 2d. each including the costs in each case. We hope this case will be a warning to other boys in the neighbourhood.

At the Crystal Palace:

1856: First fountain display, attended by Queen Victoria.

1857: First Handel festival on centenary of composer's death.

1860: First of the great band festivals.

1861: Blondin performs a spectacular rope walk.

1889: Activities and institutions included: Balloon ascent by Captain Dale; a skating rink; promenade concerts; 'A Marine Aquarium with 38 tanks well stocked with living wonders of the mighty deep'.

1911: The Crystal Palace Company's financial crises showed the affection in which the Palace was held. The Lord Mayor of London, David Burnett, led the nation to buy the Palace and, just before the First World War, it became national property.

1936: The Palace destroyed by fire; 600 local people lost their jobs.

From the *Beckenham Journal*:

April 1878: Stone Throwing In The Parish Lane. Three boys named Alfred Brooker, aged 15 . . . Frederick Wetherill aged 14 years . . . William Barrett aged 11 . . . were summoned before . . . for throwing stones, and damaging the public building on the corner of Edward Road . . . sentenced to pay 9s. 6d. or in default seven days imprisonment in Maidstone Goal. . . . Brooker was removed in custody, but Barrett's fine, made to prevent so young a boy going to prison, was kindly paid for him, this time, by Rev . . . Daukes.

June 1878: The 'Rapid' coach . . . makes the road journey daily between . . . West Wickham, and Charing Cross.

March 1941: Stanley Brown of Witham Road S.E. 20, did voluntary work, all night, at Beckenham Hospital and at 7.25 a.m. was stopped on his way home for having no lights on his bike. He was fined 15 shillings.

September 1941: The Government is anxious that the fullest use is made of this season's blackberry crop. . . . It is hoped that parties of school children, boy scouts and girl guides will help gathering in the crop . . . picker's price 3d per lb.

These notes and extracts give some colour to the local scene. In the following chapters I have endeavoured to give a fuller picture of what is a vast canvas.

David R. Johnson, 2004

1

Prehistory & History

Mr Case, site foreman at the Crystal Palace, discusses restoration with Len Brooker in 1950. Like the coryphodon, millions of years earlier, this Irish elk is also extinct. This species may have met its end with the arrival of humans. All the models or sculptures are fortunately now nationally listed 'buildings'. *(BB)*

Five London boroughs meet on the first high ridge less than 7 miles due south of the City of London. The inspiring views from this hill, at points 365 feet in height, include the centre of London to the north, the North Downs to the south and the Queen Elizabeth II Bridge, at Dartford, to the east. The views and the immediate beauty of the area were reasons for building the 'Palace of the People' on this spot. The name of the hill and the area is often given as 'Crystal Palace'. Although it is used as an address no such place is recognised as a postal district by Royal Mail, but 'Crystal Palace' apparently has a reputation that is everlasting, and the name will stay.

The name is convenient for describing this area which has a history from a time when the complication of borough borders did not exist. Crystal Palace was only used as a name of a place from the mid-nineteenth century. Likewise other local places have changed names completely or have been modified. West Norwood was once Lower Norwood, Anerley only existed as a place name some years after the railway station was so named. The whole of Anerley and part of Upper Norwood for administrative purposes were within Penge and were called Penge for centuries. Postal districts were created by the Post Office in the latter half of the nineteenth century and portions of Penge were thereafter known by their postal names. Penge, however, is the oldest local name with roots going back to the people that lived here before and during Roman times and were here when the Jutes, Saxons or Germanic peoples arrived.

The name was adopted by the Anglo-Saxons and is recorded as Penceat. The great-grandson of Alfred the Great, King Eadwig, in AD 957 granted one of his loyal thegns, Lyfing, inter alia 'Penceat', a wood '7 miles, 7 furlongs and 7 feet around'. Penceat, which would sound like Penkeat to English speakers, is analysed as Pen[n]; a hill, and ceat; a wood, by Dr Cavill of the English Place Name Society. Other sources give other shades of meaning, for 'Pen' in modern Welsh is 'head' in English. There is no doubt that the word is Celtic and has a similar meaning to nearby Forest Hill. Norwood may be a later name that partially replaced Penceat. Norwood, or wood north of Croydon, included all or parts of today's South Norwood, Upper Norwood, Penge and Dulwich.

In the Saxon charter of AD 957, the size of Penceat is indicated as about four times the size of the area which was Penge Urban District between 1899 and 1965. In 1066 Penge was part of Battersea and belonged to King Harold, who fought and died bravely at the Battle of Hastings. The lands belonging to the dead king passed to the Conqueror. In 1067 William the Conqueror granted lands, which included Penceat, to the Abbot of Westminster, for the redemption of Edward the Confessor's regalia, which had been deposited with the Abbey. The reference was, 'Moreover I have granted to them all the hunting of the wood Penceat'.

Hunting indicates a larger area than the square mile of Penge existing in the nineteenth and twentieth centuries. At the end of William's reign the Domesday Book mentions under Battersea 'a wood for 50 hogs of pannage', which is almost certainly Penge. There is no indication of a population until 1200 when there are legal records showing that there is habitation. These records increase with time and in one there is mentioned a family called De Penge. Today nearly all the people with the surname 'Penge' in Britain are first or second generation French or Italian. No one knows whether or not any of them are descended from the recorded, possibly Norman, De Penge.

During the sixteenth century the Church lost much of its land and power. The religious and administrative upheaval also left the borders of parishes uncertain. To re-establish borders, special courts were set up and people such as the oldest inhabitants were questioned. There are hundreds of files at the Lambeth Local Archives concerning the borders around Penge. It is almost certain that borders did not return to those of pre-Reformation times.

Certain parts of commons had been enclosed before the eighteenth and nineteenth centuries but most took place at this time. In the area we are dealing with, the land allocated and bought by already rich landowners in the nineteenth century was prime building land. Enrichment seems to have been the motivation for promoting Acts of Parliament to enclose land in some cases, rather than the stated 'agricultural improvement'. Once commons were enclosed, or fenced, the poor could not, for example, collect wood for cooking and heating.

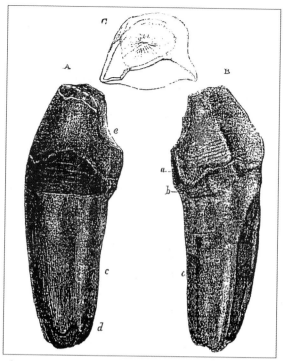

The incisor tooth, 7cm long, of a coryphodon. This 1841 find was reported variously as on Camberwell, Dulwich, Westwood, Penge and Sydenham commons. In fact, the location of the find is near to the 'Dartmouth Arms Station', today's Forest Hill railway station. A pub by this name still exists and there are claims that part of it originally served as a waiting room. The fossil was at a depth of 160ft, about 50m, in a layer from the early Eocene Age. This dates the find to an extinct animal living 55 million years ago. *(BMNH)*

An unknown eighteenth-century writer sums it up in the lines:

> The law doth punish man or woman
> Who steals the goose from off the common
> But lets the greater felon loose
> That steals the common from the goose.

In the case of the Penge Common Enclosure Act of 1827, allocation of land was made in 1837, the railway arrived in 1839 and the building of the Crystal Palace started nearby in 1852. The Crystal Palace building stood partly in Penge and partly in Dulwich Woods, Camberwell, but for various reasons it was normally described as in Sydenham or Norwood. Most of the building stood in Penge. The pictures that follow will make the story of the area clearer.

The fossil tooth on p. 9 was found during the sinking of a well. In the nineteenth century it was recorded as the tooth of a lophidon.

Scientists at the British Museum subsequently re-classified the tooth as belonging to a coryphodon, an extinct hoofed animal. It is illustrated by Michael Long, who is thanked for permission to reproduce it. (*Mammal Evolution*, by Savage & Long, British Museum) (*BMNH & ML*)

At first it was thought that the tooth belonged to an animal such as these awaiting restoration. Today these animals are not considered to be in the same family as the coryphodon. Other remains of hot and cold climate mammals have been found within 10 miles of Crystal Palace and some can be seen in the Natural History Museum.

These restored models now seem ready to graze or swim. The only other remains of large animals found within a couple of miles of the Crystal Palace Park are hippopotamidia, on the banks of the Ravensbourne near Southend Ponds. Over the last 120,000 years, the local land has not significantly changed its river systems, although there were hot, cold, dry and wet periods. The various ice sheets did not reach this far south and did not change local river routes. It is not a hot period now and a hippopotamus is not likely to cross your path when you next visit the shops.

George Brooker on the left and Victor Martin engaged on renovation work in the 1950s. The animals are arranged in time order, starting with the earliest nearer to Crystal Palace station and ending near the Penge entrance. This is the way most people would have progressed when they paid to visit the Palace. Today most people reverse the chronological order because the convenient car parks are near the Rangers' Offices and the Penge entrance. *(BB)*

Prehistoric animals are part of our local scene. They constituted an outdoor court to supplement the many 'courts' inside the Crystal Palace. This 'court' in Crystal Palace Park is the only one left to us. It is a strong reminder of the educational aims of the 1854 Crystal Palace. Prince Albert and Queen Victoria visited this local attraction on many occasions. Here, in 2002, the Duke of Edinburgh views the newly refurbished models. *(LBB)*

A Roman soldier's discharge diploma was found on Sydenham Common and handed to the British Museum in 1813. The Romano-British find was made of copper alloy and this second-century retired soldier could have gained land here. Although his name is missing we do know that he was not recruited from near Rome but from the Roman Empire north of the Alps, and that he served 25 years in the army. The diploma gives him permission to take a wife and bestows Roman citizenship, which was a very valuable right. *(BM)*

The copper alloy figure of a snake was found at the same time and place as the soldier's discharge diploma, and was also donated to the British Museum in 1813. The symbol may be related to Asklepius, the Greek god of medicine and healing. A snake is used as a symbol in the medical world today. 'In the pagan Greco-Roman world snakes . . . seldom inspired . . . fear. . . . Instead, they were usually regarded as beneficent.' From *Doctors and Diseases in the Roman Empire*, by Dr Ralph Jackson (BM Press 1988). *(BM)*

Wood was harvested from the Great North Wood for shipbuilding, especially after Henry VIII had established his yards at Deptford. The wood for the *Revenge* is said to have come from near where Norwood Park is today. The *Pelican* – later renamed the *Golden Hind* – is said to have had a similar origin. This craft, in which Drake sailed round the world, was in the time of Elizabeth I a 'tourist attraction' at Deptford, where the ship eventually deteriorated. A local man, John Davies of Camberwell parish, the Keeper of Naval Stores at Deptford, had the remaining timbers made into chairs. In 1662 he gave this one to the Bodleian Library at Oxford where it can be seen today.

The once-rural country of today's south London suburbs brings a colourful picture to mind when Rocque's 1745 map is examined. The woods shown are remnants of the Great North Wood stretching from today's South Norwood to Dulwich Wood and northwards. Part of Croydon and Penge commons are contiguous. The roads do not follow today's pattern and 'Wind Mill Hill' suggests at least one mill in or near the Upper Norwood of today. The map shows the eastern edge of Surrey which includes Dulwich and Penge. *(UNL)*

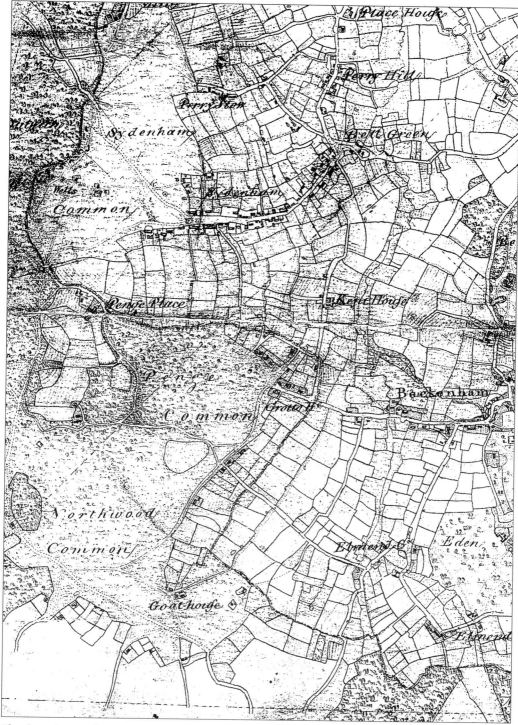

The first thorough Ordnance Survey required by the government was made at the end of the eighteenth century. Accuracy was required since the defence of the realm was the concern of the day. The thicker line is the border between Surrey and Kent with 'Penge Common' in Surrey. (BPL)

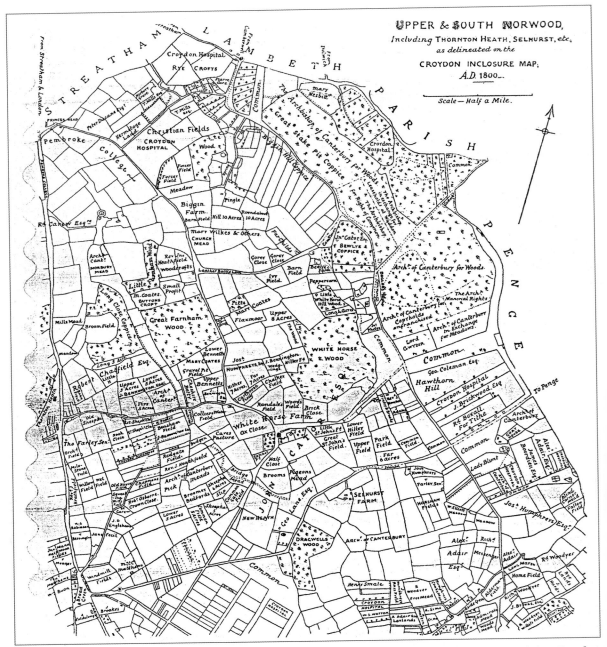

The Archbishop of Canterbury holds 'Great Stake Pit Coppice' at mid-point and near the top of this Croydon enclosure map of 1800. This is the area from which timber is reputed to have been taken to build Tudor ships such as the *Revenge*. The illustration is taken from *The Great North Wood* by J.C. Anderson, 1898.

Sydenham Common. This 1812 painting by James Pringle was completed shortly before the common was physically enclosed. The view is from the top of Kirkdale with the woman and coach proceeding down that road. The canal reservoir is on the left. The adjoining commons of Croydon, Penge and Sydenham were wooded in parts but also provided pasture for animals. Mr Colfe, the Vicar of Lewisham in the early seventeenth century, saved the common for the poor. In 1810 an Act was passed to enclose the common and there was no Mr Colfe to oppose the enclosure. Wells Park is a reminder of the green area lost. *(CL)*

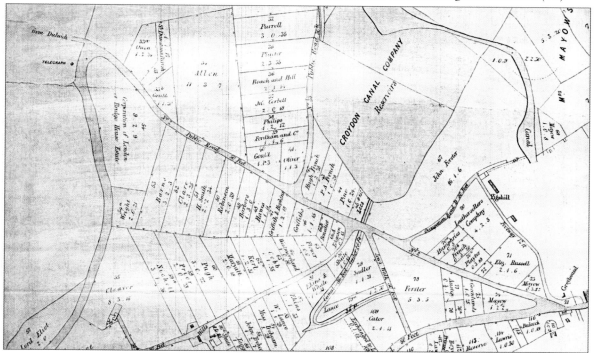

The 1819 award enclosing Sydenham Common has names such as Cator and Lawrie, which were later used for road names. The names may not be entirely clear; however, the word 'Telegraph' on the top left is discernible. This is where the artist James Pringle set up his easel for the picture above, which is looking south-east from this point. The roads on the map are marked with minimum widths which are, in most cases, the same today. The Act did bequeath us some wide main roads. *(LL)*

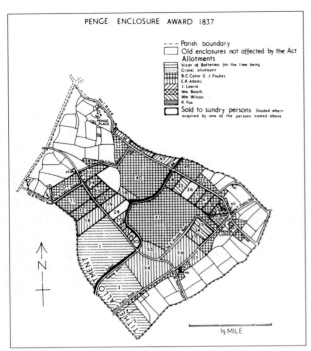

PENGE ENCLOSURE AWARD 1837

---- Parish boundary
☐ Old enclosures not affected by the Act
Allotments
Vicar of Battersea for the time being
Gravel allotment
B.C.Cator & J.Foukes
E.R.Adams
J. Lowrie
Wm Booth
Wm Wilson
R. Fox
Sold to sundry persons Shaded where acquired by one of the persons named above

½ MILE

Commons all over the country had already been enclosed, including Sydenham and Croydon, when the Act for enclosure of Penge Common was passed in 1827. This was as a result of a petition by John Cator. It took ten years to make the award to the various landowners. The first enclosure petition for Penge Common was made to Parliament fifty years earlier. Penge was exceptional both for the time it took and its late date. There had been much opposition from the Vestry and some latterly from the Lord of the Manor of Battersea, Earl Spencer. Dr B. Taylor shows that a large amount of land at both ends of Penge 'Common' had already been enclosed by non-parliamentary means before the act of 1827. (BPL)

A view from where the Crystal Palace was to be built shows Penge Place to the left and its grounds, stretching down towards Penge Church, in the centre. No closer picture of the house, at least twice the size of Beckenham Place, has so far been found. The men are clearing the top site in 1852 and below are meadows which have been enclosed farmland for centuries. Paxton lived at Penge Place before it was demolished for his new Crystal Palace grounds. (LJ)

Battersea Church, unusually placed immediately next to the Thames, is shown in records to be supported by the parishioners living in Penge 7 miles away. From Anglo-Saxon times until 1855, Penge was a detached part of Battersea. Some authorities consider that the area between the two parts of Battersea were linked as a continuous area; however, detached higher ground was often allocated to low-lying places, such as Battersea, to provide timber and animal pastures. From 1067 to the dissolution of the monasteries in the 1530s Battersea, including Penge, was owned by Westminster Abbey so that this abbey, central to British life, was supported by whatever small levy was placed on Penge. (DRJ)

This original Battersea border post stood in Lansdowne Place, Upper Norwood, from 1854, as shown on the post, until around the turn of the twenty-first century. No one appears to remember it or know where it has gone. It seems a deplorable act to remove this unique reminder of the area's link with Battersea. Please inform the author if you know where it might be.

There are many interesting views from the high ground around the Crystal Palace. Books sometimes aver that the Crystal Palace was built at the same height as the top of the cross of St Paul's; however, this does not mean that the hill is on a level with St Paul's. This view of the City from Westow Hill is photographed from a height of 365ft, the often-quoted height of St Paul's Cathedral, visible in the picture. This height is from the St Paul's churchyard pavement level to the top of the cross. St Paul's Cathedral stands on Ludgate Hill 55ft high, so that we are not at the same level on Westow Hill or on the 365ft high Crystal Palace ridge. The top of the cross is 420ft above sea level. Thanks to Robert Crayford of St Paul's architectural staff for this information. *(RP)*

Opposite, top: This artist's impression of the top of Penge Hill dominated by the Crystal Palace, built 1852–4, is incorrect. It is an impressive painting but the fountains shown are from the artist's imagination. Paxton wanted fountains that would outshine those at the palace of Versailles. The square towers were built as shown but they were not strong enough to hold the water required. The structure began to creak as the tanks were being filled, so this operation was stopped and the fountains never operated with water from these towers. Later Brunel came to the rescue. *(EP)*

Opposite, bottom: Westow Hill, *c.* 1900. This scene seems peaceful when compared with the often gridlocked mechanical congestion of a century later. Brunel's tower can be seen in the distance. Here Lambeth is on the left and Croydon on the right. The first building on the right is the Woodman Inn and associated with it is the Crystal Palace Livery Stables. There were many such stables providing servicing for horses, at one time of course the general means of road transport. *(DRJ)*

The summer palace shows the scars of eighty-two years. The northern part of the buildings, to the right of the picture, was removed by high winds in 1861 and a fire in 1866. Worse was to come on Monday 30 November 1936 when fire destroyed most of the main building. This massive fire was visible from an aircraft crossing mid-channel from Paris as well as from such distant points as the South Downs. *(EP)*

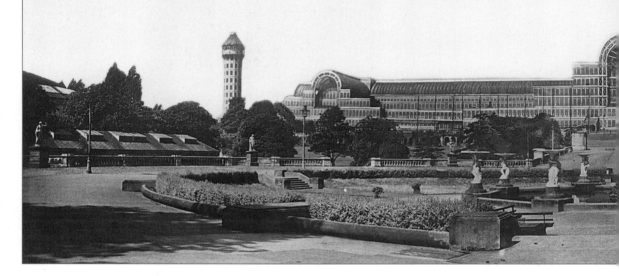

The destruction is shown in this winter picture. The remaining portion was unsafe and was pulled down. Nevertheless the 'Versailles' gardens with their graceful classical statues remained attractive until 1939 when they could no longer be maintained. The grounds continued to be used for sports, except during the war years. *(EP)*

This public house was named after Queen Adelaide, widow of William IV, who gave her royal support to the Watermen and Lightermen's Almshouses, directly across the road from here. The stables at the back of the inn were used to house all sorts of circus animals for the Penge Empire Theatre.

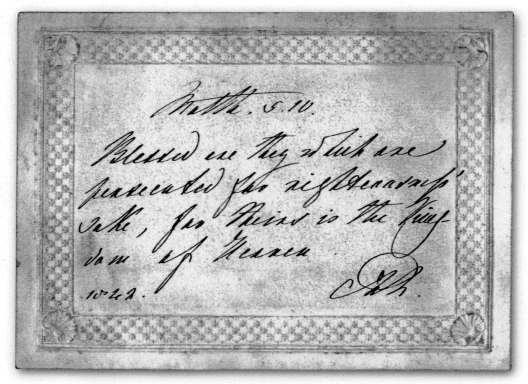

This is a facsimile of Queen Adelaide's handwriting and reflects her strong religious nature. She was a great friend to Penge since she caused another 'asylum', or alms establishment, to be built here later in the 1840s. The second was in memory of her husband William IV, who died in 1837. *(BPL)*

The venue for the first-ever public engagement of the Earl and Countess of Wessex was to a place widely described as Crystal Palace district. It was the former Railway Tavern, Anerley Station Road, now converted to the 'Streetwise' youth project, as shown on the plaque. Streetwise was established to help people under twenty-five with housing, health, employment and law.

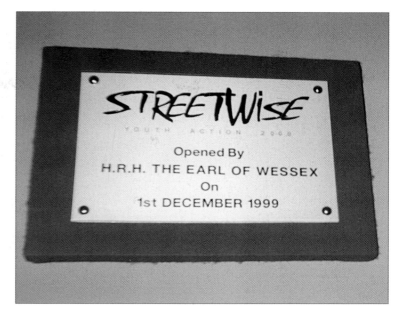

The royal couple meet people who helped this project part-funded by the Crystal Palace Partnership and the Local Housing Association. On the left of the picture is Tony Elliston, Chief Executive, Youth Action UK. Sue Polydorou, the Mayor of Bromley, is between the Earl and the Countess, and to the right of the Countess in order are Sally Hashemi, Project Co-ordinator, Councillor Chris Gaster and Virginia Harman. The Countess surprised everyone by expertly potting a ball in a game of pool.

A mountain near a sign for Penge – how could this be? This is Limpopo, formerly Northern Province, South Africa. Originally there was a farm here named after our local Penge. Amosite outcrops were discovered here in 1910 and later in that same century the major part of the world's amosite asbestos was mined here. Local place names are to be found around the world, especially in Commonwealth countries. *(HJ)*

2

Transport

Anerley station bridge. This 1906 scene is recognisable in the early twenty-first century. The future Mrs Beeton of cookery book fame would regularly meet her husband-to-be here in their courting days. Penge Town Hall in Anerley Road is behind the policeman on the left. *(JG)*

Local rivers, much larger than those of today, provided transport in prehistoric times. In the sixteenth century Queen Elizabeth is said to have sailed up the now all but vanished River Effra, which at one time flowed through Dulwich. We are certain that a Roman road cut through Lewisham, Sydenham, Beckenham and West Wickham. Evidence of Roman occupation has been found very near the Crystal Palace. The eighteenth and nineteenth centuries saw some improved roads, like those of the New Cross Turnpike Trust. Bromley, Beckenham and Croydon are known to have had scheduled transport early in the nineteenth century using Turnpike Trust roads.

Apart from 'Trust' roads private roads were built. Mr Morgan of Penge Place, which stood near the twenty-first-century Crystal Palace Park Concert Bowl, built a road over Penge Hill into Dulwich in 1789, called Morgan's Road. The Dulwich College Governors acquired the road in 1809 and erected the Penge Turnpike on this road which they renamed Penge Road. It is College Road today, the only toll road in London.

Other privately constructed toll roads existed locally. Roads between Penge and Sydenham, in most of the nineteenth century, were private and tolls were therefore payable to pass through gates. One was in what is now Kent House Road and another on the Harding's Lane and Newlands Park route. This latter was the property of Mr Harding whose name lives on in the road he once owned.

The Croydon Canal of 1809–36 was the genesis of local transport that led to the building of the Crystal Palace in the southern suburbs of London. It was authorised by Act of Parliament in 1801 to protect naval supplies as part of Britain's defence against France. About this time a canal to Portsmouth was proposed, because heavy losses had been experienced on the sea route. Britain's water-conveyed supplies

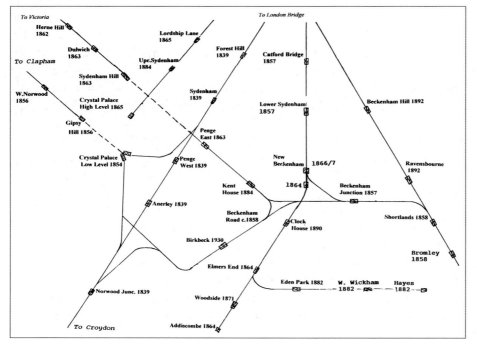

The decision to rebuild the Crystal Palace on Penge Hill in 1852 was largely influenced by the existence of the 1839 railway to Croydon. In its turn the Palace attracted residents to this area early in the spread of suburbia. The map shows when railway stations were opened, indicating the influence of the Palace and where people chose to live. (PK&NK)

The rivers to the east of the Crystal Palace ridge feed into the Ravensbourne whose outlet to the Thames is at Deptford Creek. This was the start of the river route to Lewisham, Beckenham and Bromley, probably negotiated by small craft. The creek mouth could take larger ships for building or docking, as indicated in this nineteenth-century picture. Just to the west Henry VIII established a royal dock. The *Golden Hind* was visited here by Elizabeth I in 1581 and the captain, Francis Drake, was given a knighthood. The timbers of the *Golden Hind*, like those of the *Revenge*, reputedly came from the Great North Wood. The *Revenge* was captained by Drake in the defeat of the Spanish Armada. *(LJ)*

would be safe on the Thames to Portsmouth canal. Victory at Trafalgar eventually removed the danger and made the canal unnecessary. However, a canal to Croydon looked commercially viable. Delays in its construction were caused by indecision on the type of canal and the route. One abandoned plan was for a longer route along the Ravensbourne valley and through Woodside. The investors looked for a profitable return and decided on the shorter option which was along the side of the Forest Hill, Sydenham Hill and Penge Hill ridge. It required twenty-six locks to climb the hill and there were two locks near Croydon. This slowed traffic and made it less commercially attractive. The canal was unprofitable and was sold for £40,250 to the London & Croydon Railway Company in 1836. It was a ready-made channel for part of their railroad. The railway was opened on 1 June 1839, and scheduled services started on the 5th, one of London's, and the world's first suburban railways.

The stations included the Dartmouth Arms (now Forest Hill), Sydenham, Penge, Anerley and the Jolly Sailor (now Norwood Junction). The Croydon line enabled local people to work in London but it was used at least equally for pleasure purposes. The beautiful hilly country and the railway provided the conditions for a property boom along its route.

MEASURED from LONDON BRIDGE. | **LONDON TO CROYDON.** | THROUGH LEWISHAM and BECKENHAM.

SOUTH END. Between South End and Beckenham, Beckenham Place, *John Cator*, Esq.

BECKENHAM. Kelsey Park, Sir *John Ord*; Eden Farm, Mrs. *Wildman*; Langley Farm, — *Colville*, Esq.; Langley Park, *E. Goodheart*, Esq.; and Langley Lodge, ———.

STROUD GREEN. Shirley House, and Cold Harbour, or Spring Park, *John Maberly*, Esq.; beyond which is Addington Palace, Archbishop of *Canterbury*.

ADDISCOMBE. Addiscombe Place, now a seminary of cadets for the East India Company; and

CROYDON. Birdhurst Lodge, Mrs. *Davis*.

From Croydon		From London
	From the Surrey Side of	
$13\frac{3}{4}$	London Bridge *to*	
	South End, *Kent*,	
$6\frac{1}{4}$	*page* 11	$7\frac{1}{2}$
	Forward to Bromley $2\frac{1}{2}$ *m.*	
$4\frac{3}{4}$	*To* Beckenham ☞	9
	☜ *to Bromley* $1\frac{1}{2}$ *m.*	
$3\frac{3}{4}$	Elmer's End	10
2	Stroud Green, *Surrey*	$11\frac{3}{4}$
1	Addiscombe	$12\frac{3}{4}$
	* *CROYDON, the*	
	Hospital	$13\frac{3}{4}$

BECKENHAM. The church is a neat edifice, containing many monuments; among which, on a slab in the chancel, is a remarkable brass in memory of a female who died in 1563: she is represented in a flowered petticoat, hanging down to the feet, having the sleeves slashed at the shoulders. On the monument of Mrs. Jane Clarke are some elegant lines, written by the poet Gray.

CROYDON, entrance of the town, at $1\frac{1}{4}$m. distance, Beddington Park, Mrs. *Ann Paston Gee*; beyond which is Carshalton House, *William Reynolds*, Esq.; and Carshalton Park, *John Taylor*, Esq.; and just through the turnpike, at the end of the town, Haling Park, *Charles Burnett*, Esq.

MEASURED from LONDON BRIDGE | **LONDON TO BECKENHAM, CONTINUED TO BROMLEY.** | THROUGH CAMBERWELL and DULWICH.

CAMBERWELL, at the foot of the hill, Mrs. *Perkins*.

DENMARK HILL, *Isaac Goldsmid*, Esq.; *Ralph Ricardo*, Esq; and *Richard Oakley*, Esq. At the two Lodges, *J. Fisher*, Esq.; and *D. Gordon*, Esq.

DULWICH, entrance of, Mrs. *Clarke*; entrance of the common, *C. F. Hennings*, Esq.

DULWICH, delightful for its rural simplicity, has several fine walks in its neighbourhood, which lead to elevated spots, whence very beautiful prospects are enjoyed; but it is more particularly celebrated for its college, which was founded in 1614, by Mr. Edward Alleyne, an actor in the reign of Queen Elizabeth, and the principal performer in many of Shakspeare's plays. The original edifice was erected after a plan of Inigo Jones, in the old taste, and contains the chapel and master's apartments in the front, and the lodgings of the other inhabitants in the wings. A new building was attached to this college about 10 years since, for the reception of a very valuable collection of paintings, obtained on the Continent, under peculiarly favourable circumstances, by the late Noel

From Bromley		From London
	From the Surrey Side of	
$10\frac{3}{4}$	London Bridge *to the*	
$9\frac{3}{4}$	Elephant and Castle	1
9	Walworth, *Turn pike*	$1\frac{3}{4}$
$8\frac{1}{4}$	Camberwell, *The Tiger*	$2\frac{1}{2}$
	☜ *to Peckham* $\frac{3}{4}$ *m.*	
	To Vauxhall Bridge $1\frac{1}{2}$ *m.* ☞	
$7\frac{3}{4}$	Champion Hill, *The Fox*	3
6	Dulwich, *The College*	$4\frac{3}{4}$
$5\frac{1}{4}$	Penge Turn pike	$5\frac{1}{2}$
4	Croydon Canal	$6\frac{3}{4}$
	Penge Common,	
$3\frac{1}{4}$	*The Crooked Billet*	$7\frac{1}{2}$
$1\frac{3}{4}$	Beckenham, *Church, Kent*	9
$\frac{3}{4}$	Clay Hill	10
	* *BROMLEY*	$10\frac{1}{4}$

DULWICH, descending the hill, Cassino, *C. Hammersley*, Esq.; entrance of Dulwich, *J. P. Musprat*, Esq.; *C. Clarke*, Esq.; *R. H. Clarke*, Esq.; *J. Hallet*, Esq.; *F. Schroeder*, Esq. At Ireland Green, Brockwell Hall, *J. Blades*, Esq.; and farther to the right, Tulse Hill, Dr. *Edwards*.

DULWICH COLLEGE, near, Mrs. *Rougmont*; and on the common, *J. Whitfield*, Esq.; *G. Harris*, Esq.; and Hall Place, *D. Stow*, Esq.

PENGE TURNPIKE, beyond, Kings Wood, *W. Vizard*, Esq.

CLAY HILL. *T. P. Courtenay*, Esq.

Desenfans, Esq., and presented to the institution by Sir F. Bourgeois, with the hope of thereby laying the foundation of a national gallery, where the student might at all times resort to contemplate the productions of the best masters. The paintings may be viewed every day in the week, Friday and Sunday excepted: and the hours of admission, from April to November, are from ten till five; and from November to April, from eleven till three.

The royal family, even Queen Victoria's carriage, had to pay tolls here. An outraged superintendent of police, as a result, tried to take out a summons against the lessee of the gate but he had no legal backing and failed. Royalty had to continue to pay tolls. This was called Penge Road in the mid-nineteenth century and is now College Road, the only toll road in London.

Daniel Paterson's *Road Book* of 1824 gives a good description of the villages and towns. Notice the 'Penge Turn-pike' and the bridge over the canal. The road from Southend to Stroud Green, near Croydon, was an extension in 1764 of the New Cross Turnpike Trust.

The toll gate was positioned near the first lamp-post on the right in what is now called Newlands Park. At that time the border of Beckenham and Lewisham was at the same place as now, about a quarter of a mile from Sydenham Bridge. This photograph of about 1900, some forty years after the road was made toll free, shows the middle-class homes being served by tradesmen with their carts. *(NTC)*

The Croydon Canal, seen here in 1831, had twenty-six locks at its northern end and two near Croydon. From Sydenham Bridge it was possible to boat both ways for several miles without encountering a lock. This led to a flourishing tourist trade through attractive scenery. A decorated barge left Sydenham for the opening ceremonies on 23 October 1809 to a 21-gun salute. The proprietors then boated to Croydon and dined at the Greyhound, where the chorus of their song was: 'Long down its fair stream may the rich vessel glide, And the Croydon Canal be of England the pride.' *(LJ)*

The canal narrows in this 1820 picture by James Bourne showing 'Penge Bridge' with part of John Scott's wharf on the western bank: all wharves were on this side of the canal. This was the only wharf mentioned in the opening ceremony report so must have been one of some importance. It was later called Beckenham Wharf. The tow-path was on the east side of the canal for its whole length. *(JG)*

Allowing for artistic licence this could be 'Penge Bridge' as described. The canal did make a curve to the east around what is the Homebase store today. This drawing of 1820 by James Bourne would have been completed from what is now the western side of Oakfield Road. *(JG)*

Anerley did not exist when this scene was painted in about 1830 and is given as a location to help the reader place it. In modern terms we would be looking at the back gardens of Anerley Park Road. James Dixon School would be on the left of the picture and Anerley Road would ascend the hill on the horizon. At the time of the painting this was Penge Common, and it shows the wooded nature of the sloping ground, with mature trees growing on London clay. Deep-rooted oaks flourished on this soil. Thus there was timber for ship building and good conditions prevailed for the production of charcoal, as in the rest of the Great North Wood. This industry had ended here by 1800. The enclosure of neighbouring commons in about 1800 meant that the gipsies had to find living space elsewhere. Penge Common was enclosed later, in 1837, under an Act of 1827. In 1830 the 'Swarthy Tribe', as they were described at the time, could find a haven in parts of Penge. To the right of the picture a typical gipsy shelter is visible.

There is no location given for this swing bridge painted by James Bourne. Thirty such bridges are recorded in the length of the canal along with seven 'road bridges'. The topography indicates a point in South Norwood with the Great North Wood or Penge Hill and wood in the background. This type of bridge was mainly used by farm vehicles. *(JG)*

The canal was used extensively for pleasure and undoubtedly it was a big attraction and success for boating, fishing, skating and swimming. Its intended purpose was commercial, using barges 60ft long and 9ft wide. The journey from Croydon to the end of the canal in Deptford was about 9 miles and could be completed in a day. Living accommodation was not needed and there was plenty of space in the 35-ton craft to carry bulky goods. Bricks for the expanding London and Croydon suburbs were manufactured near the canal and carried in both directions. There were thirty-seven such privately owned barges for sale when the canal closed commercially in 1836. It continued for a year in the hands of the railways and parts were used for leisure purposes. *(JG)*

Penge Common, 1820. James Bourne, the artist, has possibly painted an over-steep west bank. This picture shows the shape of the canal just to the east of what is Anerley Road today. The open ground in the background is the area between Oakfield Road and Maple Road. The standard width of the canal specified by its designer, Rennie, was 35ft tapering to 24ft; the depth 5ft. There were variations, and maps show a much broader width to the north of the Anerley Hotel, now the Anerley Arms. *(JG)*

This Tudor-style station house dating back to the mid-nineteenth century marked a spot near where the railway traversed the course of the canal it replaced. Local people took great pride in this oldest surviving suburban railway station, and assert that it was demolished over a weekend by the rail authorities, just as it was about to be listed, in 1987–8. The name Anerley was coined in 1839 by Mr William Sanderson who previously owned the land. A PO sorting office was built nearby which the officials called Anerley after the name of the nearby station. For postal purposes most of what was Penge and some of the old Beckenham parish is now Anerley. *(BL)*

This tunnel was used by the London, Brighton & South Coast Railway, successor to the London & Croydon Railway, for a regular service to the City via the East End. The same journey can be made today with a change to the Underground. Sir Marc Brunel, helped by his son Isambard Kingdom, constructed this, the first underwater tunnel in the world. It was opened as a foot tunnel in 1843 and used by the railway from 1860. The charming horseshoe-shaped entrance is typical of the early nineteenth century. Marc Brunel's invention of an excavating shield is still used for tunnelling in the twenty-first century. *(RP)*

To travel on the the 'Golden Arrow' to Paris was as prestigious in its time as a flight on Concorde. Now, alas, both have gone. The steam engine here is emerging from the tunnel under the Palace and is approaching the Crystal Palace Low Level station. This station was at one time called 'Low Level' to distinguish it from the Crystal Palace High Level station, which was closed in 1954. The signal box is marked 'Crystal Palace', indicating the change of name of this station. The normal route for this cross-channel boat train was the 'main' line from Victoria through Dulwich, Sydenham Hill, Penge East, Beckenham and so on down to the coast. *(CCK)*

This photograph was taken in 2003 from the same spot as the 'Golden Arrow' opposite. The signal-box and its staff have gone. At times it is hard to find station employees and graffiti appears, as on the wall to the right. The plant foliage seems now to be less well controlled. *(RP)*

Crystal Palace Low Level station. Steam trains are now nostalgic reminders of 'good old days', overlooking the black soot marks which they would leave on mother's washing or the back-breaking work of the fireman. A fireman shovelled coal into the engine, a job they did for perhaps 20 years before getting the better-paid job of driver. This engine is recorded as no. 772.

This listed French chateau-style tower was removed from Crystal Palace station in 1976 on grounds of 'storm damage'. At the same time it was said that those who were opposing removal, such as local historians, should pay for its repair and maintenance. Various funds have now been used to install a replica roof, so the public, indirectly, have paid for the replacement in the end!

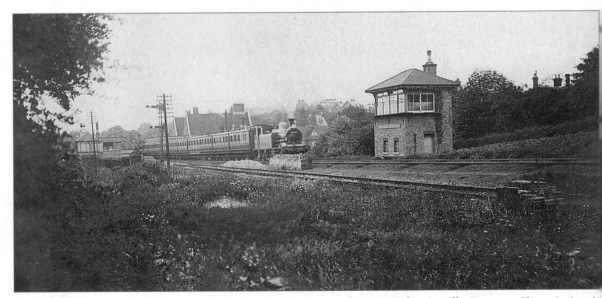

Lordship Lane station was made famous when it was painted in 1871 by Camille Pissarro. His painting is owned by the Courtauld Galleries. The line was opened on 12 June 1865 to serve the Crystal Palace at the High Level station. Lordship Lane station opened the following month. Although close to Forest Hill it was within land owned by the Dulwich College Estate, which insisted on the intricate architecture of the building. The steam engine was built in 1875 and is seen travelling towards the Crystal Palace.

The Croydon Tramlink in the twenty-first century uses some of the railway route between Beckenham and Croydon. The line from Elmers End to Addiscombe was closed on 31 May 1997. Woodside station was adapted for the new tramway, but Addiscombe station was demolished. Fortunately this photograph was taken in 1997, just in time to capture the old terminus building.

In about 1900 the stationmaster was a person of considerable importance. Penge's stationmaster 'lived over the shop' and had command of over twenty staff. Some are posed here with the boss. There was also a large goods yard to control. At Penge the stationmaster, even as late as the 1950s, would stop a fast train to allow fog-delayed commuters to board. The station is now called Penge East but is situated in Beckenham parish. (NTC)

Trams ran in some parts of south-east London until 1953 but the route shown here, through Penge High Street to the Crystal Palace Thicket Road gate, was closed by the London Passenger Transport Board in 1933, the year it was formed. The trams had been running here since 1906. The picture of about 1910 shows a tranquil world with the Crooked Billet sign as many remember it. Did all the boys shown come marching home in 1918? *(NTC)*

This view from nearly the same spot as the picture above and in about the same year shows carts pushed by men or drawn by horses, and complements the previous one since it looks in the opposite direction. Road transport was still mainly by muscle power in the first decade of the twentieth century. The scene is recognisable today with the second shop on the left performing the same function as a century ago, as a restaurant.

The butcher's shop in the centre of the picture, on the corner of Southey Street on p. 40, was Richardson's, and the twenty-first-century owners are called Glass. The site has a long history of ownership by various butchers. In the nineteenth and early twentieth centuries a slaughterhouse was operated in premises behind the shop. The picture shows the pulley needed to lift large animals. Oxen were used in transport and in farming. These and other animals would be unloaded at Penge railway station. A placid cow was kept permanently by the butcher to lead the animals from the station into a field behind the shop, in what is now Raleigh Road. The animals would be fed there until needed for fresh meat. Delivery was made to the large mansions by horse and cart. The author's grandfather had such a job.

The through service from Croydon opened on 10 February 1906 as far as the Pawleyne Arms and extended to the Thicket Road entrance to the Palace in April. The advertisement under the telegraph pole reads 'Crystal Palace, Easter Monday, Bird and Poultry Show'. The postman smoking his pipe is, no doubt, off duty.

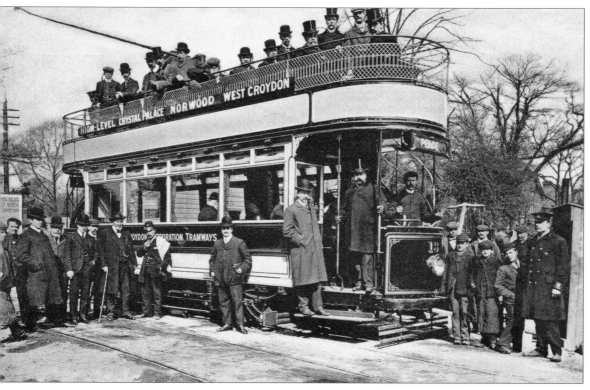

The best-known bus route from Bromley to Crystal Palace is the 227. A 229 route once existed and was sometimes confused with the 227 on a similar route. In 1934 the 229 was renumbered 254 and, between 1936 and 1939, it ran to the Palace as shown on its indicator here. In 1940 it was replaced for some of its route by the 126. This photograph was taken in Westmoreland Road, Bromley, with South Hill Wood Park in the background. Other routes still stop here. *(JH)*

A 109A bus, *c.* 1930. The 227 buses later used the same terminus and, as far as Bromley, followed the 109A route. Normally the 227 buses faced the opposite direction at the Crooked Billet stop. When the London Passenger Transport Board was formed in 1933 most of the Thomas Tilling vehicles were absorbed into their fleet. *(BM)*

The Croydon Corporation tram is new in 1906 and the official and public travellers pose for the photograph. Others are in a hurry and are blurred. The double kerbs and immediate background are still here on Anerley Hill. The local papers in about 1906 show that the upper classes living along the new routes objected to the noise of the trams and some moved away as a response. *(JG)*

In 1905–6 the disruption to traffic caused by laying the tramlines must have been minimal. Today this stretch of road is constantly busy, with pedestrian crossings to make it possible to cross the road. This scene is just above Avington Grove and the trees surrounding St John's Church can be seen across the road. The view is similar today. All behind the photographer has changed as a result of Second World War bombing and is Malcolm School playing field. (JG)

This scene of about 1938 shows a no. 654, Crystal Palace to Sutton, descending Anerley Hill with the South Tower demanding attention. Trolleybuses were first used in London in 1931. In 1936 they were used on this route, to be replaced by diesel buses in 1959. (JG)

The Crystal Palace, though burnt down in 1936, had such prestige that the surrounding district is still named after it. This no. 3 bus is in Trafalgar Square and stories are told of foreigners trekking to the mythical Crystal Palace when intrigued by bus indicator boards. Twelve bus routes terminate at Crystal Palace Parade.

3

The Crystal Palace

The 284ft in height and 46ft diameter South Tower dominates the scene above Anerley Hill. This tower and its northern counterpart had to hold 2,000 tons of water and withstand the vibrations caused when this was released to feed the fountains. This view is from about 1910 and shows the last tram stop before the vehicle was allowed to crawl up the hill to the Crystal Palace terminal. *(JG)*

The Crystal Palace building in London's southern suburbs, 1854–1936, was rebuilt partially from the material used in the the Great Exhibition of the Works of Industry of all Nations, held in Hyde Park in 1851. 'Partially' because there was need for far more building material on the hillside site; even the external glass needed was far greater than at Hyde Park. The unofficial name 'Crystal Palace' for the Hyde Park construction was first, it is thought, given by the *Punch* periodical. The title was apt and appealed to the popular imagination, and has stuck to the point that it echoes long after the second building's demise in 1936.

One popular misconception is that the 1854–1936 Crystal Palace was much larger than the Hyde Park construction. Some books quote twice or three times the size. It seems best to allow the reader to judge. A few measurements will help; comparisons are:

	Great Exhibition (Hyde Park) 1851 ft	*Crystal Palace* (South London) 1854 ft
Length	1,848	1,608
Greatest width	456	384
Height	108	173
Height (garden side)		197
Area of building sq.ft	798,912	541,440
Display area [approx] sq.ft	991,857	717,120

Joseph Paxton rose from humble and difficult circumstances to be the Head Gardener and close friend of the 6th Duke of Devonshire at Chatsworth in Derbyshire. The freedom, finance and practical experience Paxton gained there was the genesis that helped produce the Crystal Palace. Paxton improved greenhouses or 'stoves', such as the conservative or warming wall shown here. He designed and built the Great Stove at Chatsworth which was 67ft high and covered nearly an acre. This was a decade before the building of the Palm House at Kew. The Great Stove was not maintained during the First World War and had to be demolished soon afterwards.

New Crystal Palace, 1854. Two square water towers were built at about the height of the main building. The towers were not strong enough to hold water for the fountains and, in 1855, I.K. Brunel was commissioned to build the 'round', actually twelve-sided, towers always associated with the New Crystal Palace. The remains of the canal were below Minden Road a little above the bus terminal, new in 2003. The Tudor-style Anerley railway station is on the far left and the building next to it is the hotel for Anerley Gardens. *(LJ)*

In approximate figures, the cubic capacity or volume of the 1854 building was about 25 per cent greater and the display area 30 per cent less than that of the 1851 building. The figures were supplied by Ken Kiss, Hon. Acting Curator of the Crystal Palace Museum, who is thanked for his research.

The two main buildings are compared here. The towers and many other additional constructions made after 1854 would have added greatly to the building stock. The fire damage of 1866 removed the North Transept and part of the North Nave, a decrease in size that was never replaced.

The building in Hyde Park was opened on 1 May 1851 by Queen Victoria and was a temporary exhibition which closed less than six months later with a huge profit. The whole stretch of land from the Victoria & Albert Museum to the Albert Hall was purchased with part of the profits. Since Prince Albert had been a main driving force for the Crystal Palace this portion of land was named 'Albertopolis'.

The directors of the London, Brighton & South Coast Railway gave financial backing to the Crystal Palace Company in 1852 to rebuild the Palace near their line. Paxton was to be a director of the newly formed company which had purchased the Hyde Park Crystal Palace for £70,000. A site was found. Paxton said that Penge Place was 'the most beautiful spot in the world for the Crystal Palace'. It opened here on 10 June 1854.

The North Transept can be clearly seen in this photograph, dating from after the completion of Brunel's towers in 1856. The 1854 building was complex and the tall garden side, seen here, meant that the total amount of superficial glass approached twice the amount used in 1851. The fire of 1866 removed the North Transept and northern end of the main building. There was insufficient insurance to allow rebuilding. The Italian garden, with its fountains, can be seen in the foreground of the picture.

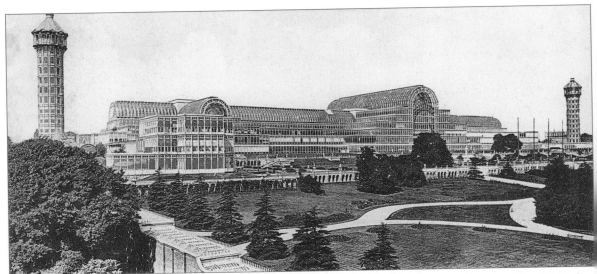

This new year card clearly shows the truncated northern end of the building as a result of the 1866 fire. The wind damage of 1861 had removed the old separate tower block, leaving another gap. This view is from about 1890, and the poles seen between the main building and the northern tower on the right are for the Brock's firework displays. The author enjoyed them sitting on a wall. Alas, the wall, with much else, was destroyed by a bomb in 1940. The ruined Palace site was bombed during the Second World War, so its life would not have extended very long after 1936.

The firework displays were provided by C.T. Brock & Co. of Sutton, Surrey, on many Thursday nights. The first one was held on 12 July 1865 with an audience of 20,000 paying to watch the spectacle. Entry could be expensive but any 'One Shilling Day' attracted big crowds. These displays were continued, with a long break around the First World War, for some seventy years. They were enjoyed free of charge if you happened to live nearby; or even 2 or 3 miles away.

South Wing. The vastness of the building along with its greenhouse function can be seen in this view which is at 90° to the picture at the top of p. 50. The ferns and flowers must have looked beautiful, reflected in the pool and falling water. The fish and foliage were killed by the fire of 30 November 1936 but amazingly, Osler's fountain was not completely consumed by the fire that destroyed the Palace.

Osler's crystal fountain. This dazzling fountain was such a success at the 1851 Palace that it was moved up Sydenham Hill and across to Penge Hill and the New Crystal Palace in 1854. The giant clock was a good advertisement for 'Dent, 61 The Strand'. Part of the back of the card reads, 'Souvenir of a happy visit to the dear old Palace, with my darling Phil'. People from far and wide had a great affection for the Crystal Palace where they had probably enjoyed a few hours away from a strenuous everyday life.

New Osler's fountain. The 1851 creation survived the fire of 1936. Such was its fame that it has been recreated to the same size by Infomart within their Crystal Palace in Dallas. Pieces of the old fountain were salvaged still with an identification number, used in the 1850s transfer. Infomart bid and obtained at auction in London a piece of the remains of the old fountain. Unfortunately their agent, a Mr Greatrex, the founder chairman of the Crystal Palace Foundation, dropped this rare object and it smashed into at least 57 pieces. This seems to illustrate how well a horse-and-cart journey did in its transfer in the 1850s. The modelling of their 1985 building on the Crystal Palace shows the longevity of the fame of this great building and some of its contents. Infomart are proud to have copied what at the time was called the 'Eighth Wonder of the World'. By kind permission of Infomart, Dallas, USA. (ID)

Abu Simbel. The inside of the Palace was arranged in a series of 'courts' depicting mostly historic times and styles of art. The original ancient Nubian monuments in Egypt were moved to safety in the 1960s when the Aswan High Dam was about to be constructed. Many will remember these statues from that time. The original Colossi were 65ft high and built by Rameses II; these were faithfully recreated in the Crystal Palace North Transept, as shown here. *(EP)*

Egyptian Court. The sense of humour expressed on this card, of *c.* 1900, possibly does not have the same connotation as today. The inscription reads 'Have just been making love to the end beauty, love Doris'. No doubt the intellect was being elevated and mind instructed as intended by the designers of the New Palace.

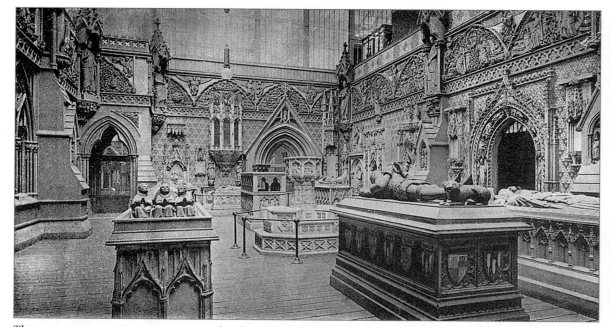

There were numerous courts created. The Medieval Court was transferred from the Hyde Park Crystal Palace. There was little opportunity in the nineteenth century for travel, even in Britain, and these courts provided a chance for the less well-off to enjoy the sights well-heeled travellers could visit. The architecture of Lincoln or Rochester cathedrals could be sampled here.

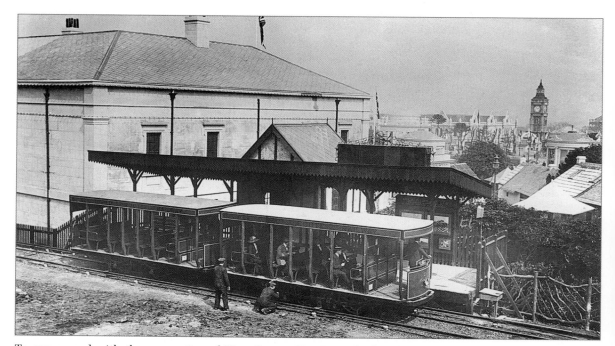

To correspond with the coronation of King George V, a Festival of Empire was held at the Crystal Palace in the summer of 1911. The line of the Red Route Railway visited stops such as Newfoundland and Canada. The replica scaled-down models of Parliament buildings were large enough to walk into and were used as barracks in the First World War.

GENERAL VIEW OF CRYSTAL PALACE,
AND CANADIAN BUILDING.

Most people throughout the life of the Palace arrived by train. Both Crystal Palace stations had covered walkways. The glass-covered long building in the foreground of this picture is the Colonnade, which led from Crystal Palace Low Level station to the Palace. It was lined with replica statues for most of its length and was about 1,000ft long. You could then walk about 1,600ft through to the north of the main building and, turning right, walk approximately another 450ft, giving an undercover walk of well over half a mile.

By the 1930s car ownership was still unusual. Perhaps those who were wealthy enough to own a car could also afford the more expensive entry days. No problems then with parking along the Crystal Palace Parade, which seventy years later is illegal. The buses are near the Crystal Palace fire station. After 1866, as here, photographers avoided the North Wing so that its lack of symmetry was not shown. (EP)

The largest organ in the British Isles was housed in the Main Transept. It had 4,500 working pipes which at the 1936 fire were heard, through thermal currents, to be groaning out a discordant lament for the dying building. Some of the Handel Festivals had over 4,000 performers seated around the organ shown here.

Charles Haddon Spurgeon, the great preacher of mid-nineteenth-century fame, preached on 7 October 1857 to his largest congregation, nearly 24,000, inside the Central Transept, about the same area as that depicted in the Great Organ picture. He was concerned with the 'restoration of tranquillity in India' at the time of the Mutiny. He had no electronic assistance for his voice. Billy Graham also attracted large crowds on several visits to this country. This one was at the Crystal Palace Sports Stadium on 23 June 1989, during 'Mission 89'. *(RP)*

The scene looks east from near where boats could be rented, *c*. 1920. The lake was the reservoir for the water used in the fountains. The water would be pumped up to the towers from here and thus lower its level. When the fountains were operating the water would feed down into the lake and restore its level. By 1920 it was called the boating lake rather than the tidal lake, its earlier name. *(LJ)*

This view of about 1925 has Farquhar Road in the foreground followed by the High Level station, the Crystal Palace Parade and then the Palace. The oval shape is the cycle racing track and to the right part of the football ground. The large houses, top left, are on Crystal Palace Park Road, in Beckenham, but with the postal address of Sydenham.

This view of the Palace in about 1925 also shows trees all around and Dulwich Wood beyond, looking almost untouched by development. The replica of the Canadian Parliament building, constructed for the Empire Exhibition of 1911, is in the central foreground with Maxim's 'flying machine' to the right. The small building to the right of the South Tower, adjacent to Anerley Hill, is all that remains of the Palace buildings. It now performs an important function as the Crystal Palace Museum.

The Palace required constant maintenance and these men were staff renovating the roof in 1930. The leading man in the photograph is Frank Brooker who, after the Second World War, helped to renovate the sculptures of extinct animals near the tidal or boating lake. Frank and the next man, Fred Munro, lived in Woodbine Grove and the third man, Eddie Hancock, lived in Hawthorne Grove, all in Penge. The Palace brought much welcome work to its surrounding districts. (BB)

Aerial view, December 1936. The two towers and part of the Northern Nave along with other buildings were not destroyed. The firemen were not as ineffective as often portrayed. No lives were lost in this, the most spectacular south London conflagration. This was partially owing to the prompt action of Sir Henry Buckland, General Manager of the Crystal Palace, who hurried to warn members of an orchestra practising in the Garden Hall. The buildings to the east of the North Tower also survived but were destroyed by fire in 1950. *(EP)*

In about 1950 the 1854 life-size statue representations of prehistoric animals were in a poor state. Teeth were missing and paint flaking. A local Penge firm, Brooker Brothers, received the contract for renovation. George Brooker, in his nineties in the twenty-first century, is no worse for his brush with this 'monster'. The animals were sculpted by Mr Waterhouse Hawkins who lived in Belvedere Road while Director of the Fossil Department of the Crystal Palace. *(BB)*

Life at the Palace. The composite picture compresses some of the story of the place at one time affectionately called 'Auntie Crystal Palace'. The pictures date from about 1905. Some features not mentioned elsewhere in this book are: top left, 'Moses' by Michelangelo; middle top, the Rosary; top right, 'The Three Graces'; bottom left, the Topsy Turvy Railway; middle bottom, the Alhambra.

Fun, *c.* 1900. Major B.S.F. Baden-Powell, brother of the future founder of the Boy Scout movement, experimented with a winged boat which would be launched down a slide similar to the one shown at the top left. He was a member of the Aeronautical Society of Great Britain and conducted many experiments in the Palace grounds. The electric canoe featured in the picture illustrates the element of fun which attracted millions.

This is June 2003 and, as in the heyday of the Palace, a circus is here in the form of Zippo's Big Top. But elephants and other exotic animals do not feature in twenty-first-century entertainments. Just over a hundred years ago, in February 1900, an elephant called Charlie retaliated after cruel treatment, killed his keeper and escaped. The elephant traversed Penge, Beckenham, West Wickham and Hayes where he was recaptured in Barnet Wood. Later at Crystal Palace he was shot.

'Sketch on the Proposed site of the Crystal Palace', from the *Illustrated London News*, 5 June 1852.

This recent prize-winning photograph shows the remaining part of Paxton's Grand Central Walk, which is near the Penge entrance of Crystal Palace Park. The trees give a suggestion of the beauty that Hone, walking a similar path in 1829, described as 'a Cathedral of bird song'. *(CW)*

4

The Environment

A grocer's store at 31 Arpley Road in 1937, dressed for the coronation of George VI. On the opposite side of the road, nearer Penge High Street, was the entrance to Shaftesbury Hall. The hall suffered the same fate as the nearby shops in the High Street which were destroyed by a V1 flying bomb on 21 July 1944. The London City Mission worked in this road, the centre of one of the poorest areas in the district. *(SM)*

Governments, or other national organisations, can change the character of society. Often the reverse is true and what happens at local level leads on to national movements or change. Sometimes it is a mixture of both, and even international influences work both ways. The Church has had a big impact on local life even to the present multi-cultural twenty-first century. Some local factors responsible for the area's character are that the Abbots of Westminster owned Penge from 1067 to the Reformation and that the Archbishops of Canterbury held Croydon parish and had a palace there. There was also a palace for the Bishops of Rochester at Bromley. The local presence of these churchmen brought a degree of economic prosperity to the area. Their retinues and horses had to be fed and tended, and consequently local trade prospered. Long-lasting institutions such as the Whitgift and Trinity schools are also their legacy.

Wealthy landowners stamped their influence on the area and are known in the names of places and roads that we use today. In the thirteenth century a family called de la Rochell, who originated from La Rochelle in France, held Beckenham and were called Rokell in English. They and their successors had powers in the

Heroes, c. 1925. A Salvation Army bandsman seems an unlikely candidate for a hero and there are few left to bear witness. This caption records two such unsung Salvation Army heroes. This is Sidney George Norman of 121 Victor Road and the second is Harvey Stanley Wilcox of 128 Victor Road, both with the address Penge, though in fact in Beckenham parish. During the Second World War both men would do whatever they could to help during and after air attacks. Mr Norman fought to seal gas fractures and eventually, as a result of his exertions and the effects of escaping gas, died early. Mr Wilcox was in his Salvation Army uniform when he was killed by a bomb along with the Hawkes family he was comforting on the evening of 7 November 1943. (CD)

Happy evening, *c.* 1900. Social work was also performed by other church organisations. This is an HSE or Happy Saturday Evening, or PSE, Pleasant Saturday Evening. To combat the many beerhouses, community singing and general entertainment would be organised on a regular basis, especially by missions. This was inside the Alexandra Mission. (CD)

selection of local priests or the parsons who received the tithes of a parish. These rights were held by Viscount Bolingbrooke in the eighteenth century for both Beckenham and Battersea, since he was lord of the manor of both. He could therefore appoint the priests of each of these parishes. Often the rector of a parish had more than one curate to assist. Sometimes a rector would pay another to carry out all of the parish duties.

The Revd William Fraganeau was first given the living of Battersea, which included Penge, in 1758. In 1765 Bolingbrooke obtained a dispensation so that Fraganeau of Battersea could simultaneously hold the living of Beckenham. This plural holding continued until 1778 when Fraganeau died.

In the eighteenth and nineteenth centuries the Cators, the Edens, the Lennards and others lived locally and added to the buildings in the area. John Angerstein, 1735–1823, at one time owned Kent House. His collection of thirty-eight paintings, bought by the nation in 1824 for £57,000, formed the nucleus for the start of the National Gallery.

Kent House, later Kent House Farm, is described in some books as the first house in Kent 'when coming from the London area'. This is incorrect. It was named when London was 8 miles away and beyond the Thames. Between Kent House and London stood many places in Surrey including Southwark. It was the first house in Kent when approached from places like Penge, about 500 yards to the west, in Surrey.

Buildings such as almshouses were built locally because of influential people. John Dudin Brown of Sydenham, for example, caused some sixty almshouses to be built in Penge. Leo Frank Schuster of Penge Place was a director of the London, Brighton & South Coast Railway and the Crystal Palace Company (CPC). He must have had an influence on the decision of the CPC to purchase his estate for the site of the 1854 Crystal Palace. Paxton's Crystal Palace had a wide appeal and similar buildings, often called 'Crystal Palace', mushroomed around the world in the nineteenth century, especially in capital cities.

Even in the late twentieth century Paxton's architectural concepts were manifest in this 1.4 million sq. ft of working space. The brochure for this building, modelled on the Crystal Palace, shows its technological debt to the ideas of the mid-nineteenth century. Like US enthusiasm for Shakespeare, Infomart proved their admiration for creativity by their financial backing. The building is a 'look-alike . . . reborn in 1984', as they state. The nearest we have in the United Kingdom to Crystal Palace architecture is the Vilar Floral Hall of the Royal Opera House in Covent Garden, built in 1859. By kind permission of Infomart, Dallas, Texas. *(ID)*

It was a happy occasion when Penge Salvation Army Colonel, Margaret Hay, won *The Times* 'Preacher of the Year Award' in 2000. This was the first time a woman had ever won, and the contest is open to any religious group.
The judges are also from across the religious spectrum and there were over 500 entries. There was a high standard of preaching in that year. Mrs Hay, like many Salvationists, also does voluntary prison work.

The Beckenham Institute, Penge, was later called the Alexandra Hall Mission. The 1877 group of buildings provided coffee, tea and soft drinks, a library and reading room. Hot baths were available for 6d and cold baths for 3d. A little spartan by modern standards, perhaps; however, a cold bath was better than none. Social evenings were still held here until it was bombed on 20 September 1940. The author was in a nearby shelter although earlier, as a Cub Scout, he had watched the weavings of fighter planes during the Battle of Britain from the front of the building on the left. His mother, who did not seem to understand the excitement, dragged him to shelter! *(BPL)*

Leighton Street Mission in Croydon shows children badly clad and some without footwear, 1908. The London City Mission, like the Salvation Army, worked in very poor and challenging places. Soup kitchens helped in extreme cases, and dropping in for coffee and cake diverted some men from 'drowning their sorrows'. *(LCM)*

Shaftesbury Hall,
ARPLEY ROAD, PENGE.

LADS' CLASS

A SHORT
MEMORIAL Service
AND
UNVEILING OF TABLET

In memory of 76 members of the above Class who gave their lives for Home and Country in the great war, will (D.V.) take place on

Saturday, AUGUST 9th, 1919,
At 3-30 p.m.

DR. SYDNEY TURNER, J.P. will Preside,
Supported by the Clergy and Ministers of Penge, P.U.D. Councillors, and others.

G. T. HAYCRAFT, ESQ., O.B.E.
Has kindly undertaken to unveil the Tablet.

Will all the old members of the above Class accept this as an invitation to be present.

At the Arpley Road Mission the selfless and altruistic work of the missionaries of the LCM was reflected by the people who would generously help each other. Many men went off to the First World War. Those who did not return were commemorated with a memorial stone generously donated by the people of this area. The tablet was carefully rescued from the debris after the bombing of 21 July 1944 and lovingly kept by Mr Morris at 53 Arpley Road. Later, on 'slum clearance' in the mid-1970s, Bromley Council officials gave assurances of its dignified preservation. Its present location is unknown. (SM)

Celebration, 1953. The Arpley Road Queen Elizabeth II coronation procession tours the adjacent roads collecting funds for the children's party. Beckenham boys attending the grammar school in Penge were warned to 'keep well clear of the Arpley Road area', even as recently as this time. Are the legends of police patrolling in twos true? If so, no one who previously lived there remembered this when interviewed recently. (SM)

This postcard gives a good overview of Upper Norwood churches in 1900. Top right is All Saints, Church Road, the middle row from left to right is St Paul's, Hamlet Road, and next is Christ Church, Gipsy Hill. The tower seen here has been converted into homes and the church has been beautifully rebuilt to the right, mainly in Highland Road. The bottom left shows St John's, Auckland Road, and bottom right St Aubyn's.

This Saxon font has an interesting history. It was sold in 1800 by a St George's churchwarden to the landlord of the Crooked Billet in Penge, who used it as a cistern. Later it was used as part of the floor of a summerhouse at the inn until this use was reported to the Revd William Cator. He re-purchased it in 1876 for Beckenham Church, to avoid its further desecration. Penge people are recorded as having been baptised at this font at Beckenham for centuries since it was this church they attended, rather than their parish church at Battersea. The Saxon font is no longer able to hold water; it now stands in an honourable position near the Beckenham parish church entrance.

St John's Church, designed by Edwin Nash, was opened in 1849. It was the first parish church exclusively for Penge. No longer were parishioners expected to travel to St Mary's, Battersea, which had been their parish church. Beckenham parish church provided for the spiritual needs of most the inhabitants of Penge up to this time. This included loaning a curate for the chapel that was built in Penge in 1837. St John's is thought to have been so named since its main benefactor was a 'John', the same John Dudin Brown who generously helped the foundation of the neighbouring Watermen's Almshouses. *(LJ)*

Opposite, top: The church of St Paul in Hamlet Road, was built in 1866 when Penge was not a hamlet, but still often called the Hamlet of Penge. St John's parish had to be divided in two because of the population increase after the arrival of the Crystal Palace. St Paul's interior was very ornate for a Church of England building. It suffered some bomb damage in the Second World War and was eventually closed for demolition in 1971. The new church was opened in 1978 and the sign outside reads St Paul's, Penge, in 2004. *(LS)*

Opposite, bottom: Although Hamlet Road and St Paul's Church are in the postal district of Upper Norwood (SE19), the church's parish extends into Anerley (SE20). The first Vicar of St Paul's, the Revd W.H. Graham, recognised a need to reach the poorer people of his parish and accordingly a mission church was built at the junction of Casteldene and St Hugh's roads, the foundation stone being laid on 28 July 1883. The church was damaged by Second World War bombing and, although repaired, was little used. Vandals finally accomplished what the Luftwaffe had failed to do and in the 1970s, soon after this photograph was taken, it was demolished.

Like most churches locally in the late nineteenth century, St Anthony's started life as a small corrugated-iron chapel, erected in 1878. In 1898 the building had an upper floor used as a church and the lower floor as a school. In 1926 the foundation stone of the present church was laid and it opened beside the school in 1927. The debt had to be paid before consecration. This was not until 1951 when Bishop Brown conducted the ceremony. The Genoa Road Catholic Church School has expanded with additional buildings and now has 350 pupils. *(NTC)*

One of the largest complexes of church buildings locally was the Baptist church in Maple Road, Penge. It was built in 1893 to replace a building of 1867. The church could accommodate 1,100 people and it had two large auxiliary halls plus other large rooms. The building next to the nearer shops and in front of the steeple is now the church. The twenty-first-century church can accommodate about half the former number. The complex was badly damaged in the Second World War. *(LS)*

Many organisations and sports connected with the Penge Baptist church flourished, especially before the Second World War. Boxing, fencing and gymnastics were all very well provided for. They even had their own sports ground in Lennard Road, Beckenham. This picture from about 1900 shows the site of the future Baptist sports ground, starting beyond the Pool river, which is in the foreground. *(NTC)*

Anerley Methodist church held its opening service on 6 February 1879. It was destroyed in the Blitz on 18 December 1940. It had seating for 1,046, and behind this building was the old smaller church and halls, which survived the bombing. These old buildings have served well ever since. In the nineteenth and early twentieth century Girls' and Boys' Brigades were connected with this church, and since 1945 it has sponsored Scouts. The Croydon Canal originally cut through their grounds. *(NTC)*

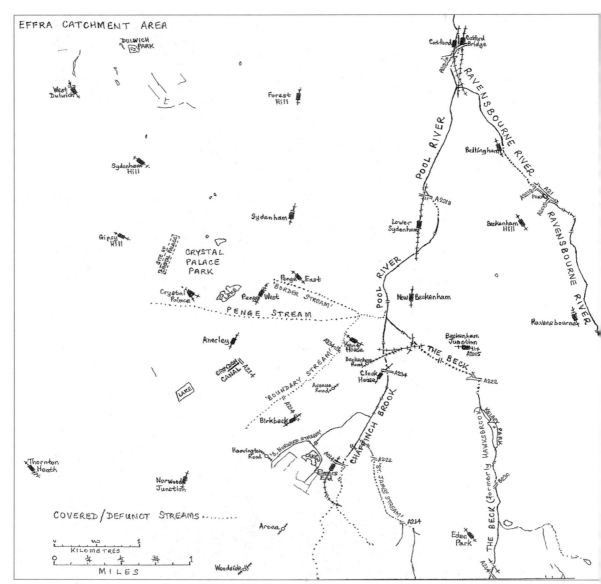

The Pool river's tributaries include the Chaffinch Brook and the Hawk's Brook or Hawkesbrook, now called the River Beck. 'Beck' is a back-formation from Beckenham, first used in about 1800. A mistaken belief exists that Beckenham derived its name from the word for a brook which is used in the north of England, i.e. 'beck'. The name Beckenham derives from the landowner in Saxon times named 'Beohha', the 'hh' being pronounced 'k' as in 'loch' when spoken by a Scot. Beohha had a 'Ham', or home and estate here. The name 'Hawk' might perhaps be considered for reinstatement; it harmonises with other local rivers named after birds, like Chaffinch and Ravensbourne, which are part of the same system. Note that the Ravensbourne and its tributaries flow generally north-westwards and are checked by the high ground stretching from the Crystal Palace northwards towards New Cross. The Pool and its tributaries run almost due north. The source of the Beck or Hawk's Brook, near Spring Park Wood, is virtually due south of Deptford Creek. (RP)

This is the 2002 troop summer activity of Scouts who are sponsored by Anerley Methodist Church. The boys over eleven thoroughly enjoyed this Midlands canal summer camp. The scout leader and his wife, Mr and Mrs Martin, were later recalled to work in Scotland and the over-eleven Scouts had no leader, the section closed and the boys went to other troops. The younger sections of this Methodist-sponsored group continue to meet at Malcolm School. *(TM)*

The Scout group still connected with the Anerley Methodists was with the YMCA before 1945. They were originally called the '1st Penge YMCA Scouts' and helped at the first ever large Scout gathering. This was held at the Crystal Palace in 1909. The food and refreshments on show were no doubt welcome. *(NTC)*

This is one of the Beckenham girls who attended the large Crystal Palace Rally. Children had formed themselves into patrols of about seven from 1908 and these patrols presented themselves to Baden-Powell (BP), founder of the Scouts.
In the case of the local girls he said 'Go and find a good woman to lead you'. Eventually the Girl Guides were formed by BP's sister with other help in 1910. *(KB)*

The first name on this memorial plaque is William Beckham, one of eight Scouts accidentally drowned in 1912. He was a promising scholar and brother to John and Edward, who were both saved from the sea in this tragedy. If Edward Beckham had drowned we would not have David Beckham, England's football captain, nine decades later; Edward Beckham was the great-grandfather of David Beckham. The plaque shows that the scouts belonged to the 2nd Walworth (Dulwich Mission) Troop of Baden Powell Boy Scouts. (BL)

Winston Churchill MP, First Lord of the Admiralty, showed his feelings for the distress of the people of south London by ordering a naval craft to take the bodies back to London. There was national interest, and crowds lined the funeral route through Camberwell and Peckham to Nunhead Cemetery. Mr Marsh, the Scoutmaster, did not continue his voluntary work, although experts and people like Mrs Beckham did not blame him. He served with distinction as a Commander in the Navy in the First World War. (BL)

Dulwich College supports a mission to the less well-off area north of Dulwich to this day. In 1912 one former Dulwich College scholar, Sidney James Marsh, 29 years old, was the Scoutmaster and skipper of this boat. He volunteered to do this work and live in the slums of Walworth with the people he served. He was motivated by the belief that because of his privileged background he owed a debt to society, and felt it was his Christian duty to help deprived youth. He had a good knowledge of water craft and had trained the Scouts in seamanship so that they won prizes for their skill. The cutter that capsized in freak weather near Sheppey is shown setting out from near the old Waterloo Bridge. *(BL)*

The 1st Crystal Palace Patrol was formed by boys in Norwood in 1908. One of these boys later reached the rank of brigadier in the Army and returned to open the present 2nd Croydon Scout Hall in Cintra Park, Upper Norwood. This is a rare original sketch by Baden-Powell made in 1929 when a member of this Crystal Palace Patrol, or Troop, was Aide-de-Camp to BP. *(LH)*

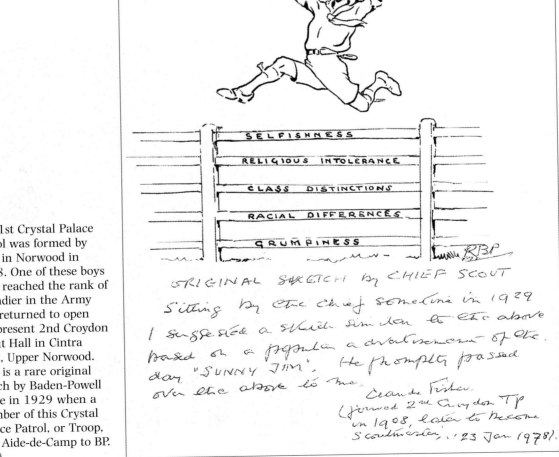

On 16 May 1840 the Lord Mayor of London paraded from Sydenham with bands playing, 'scarlet liveries, Vintners Company's watermen' and hundreds of other uniformed organisations on his way to Penge. Here he laid the first foundation brick for the almshouses, the record states. Between the road seen here and the main building a 'gallery was constructed for 500 guests including elegantly dressed ladies'. This must have been one of the most colourful parades ever seen in this, then rural, area.

The Royal Watermen and Lightermen's Asylum consists of sixty homes erected incrementally between 1839 and 1843 for aged single or married watermen or their widows. George Porter designed them in the neo-Tudor style and they are nationally listed buildings. John Dudin Brown, a Master of the Company, gave the land on which they stand and also contributed much to the cost of the building. Queen Adelaide gave £100 and consented to become patroness.

The Watermen pensioners moved from the Asylum at Penge in 1973 to their new quarters at Hastings, the 'Royal Watermen's Cottage Homes'. Their patron is now HM the Queen and they have fifty semi-detached bungalows in which to live a community life with a warden to help. The flagpole seen here, near their recreation hall, was moved from Penge. There were plans to demolish the Penge almshouses; objectors included Sir John Betjeman, and as a consequence we still have these attractive buildings.

Part of the timbers of the ship made famous by Turner's painting *The Fighting Temeraire* once rested here in the former chapel, which later became the committee room. This model, once thought to be of the *Temeraire*, was housed in a showcase definitely made of *Temeraire*'s timbers. The showcase is now held by the Watermen's Hall in London and is often displayed at events such as Henley Royal Regatta. The model is in the Watermen's Hall in London and is the largest bone model ship known. It was held at Penge because in the 1840s many living there were Trafalgar veterans. There was a strong connection with the Royal Navy and the Watermen's Company. Queen Adelaide was the patroness of the almshouses and recommended a candidate, 'Mrs Shillingford, as an object of . . . bounty'. In other words, she was to be given one of the almshouse places. Mrs Shillingford's husband had been coxswain to Nelson at the battle of Tenerife in 1797.

William IV Almshouses. Queen Adelaide in 1847 bought land from John Dudin Brown near the Watermen's Almshouses on the other side of the site of the proposed new church. These were for 'twelve widows or orphan daughters of officers of the Royal Navy'. Each house was endowed generously with £1,000. A female servant was allowed and each house had a tiny room at the back for the servant. Daughters were allowed to stay to any age; however, male children left at twelve to become midshipmen. Why the man is painted into the picture, in this female haven, is unknown. *(LJ)*

The desirable residences are now all privately owned, the foundation having moved to new bungalows near Portsmouth. The Penge almshouses opened in 1848, as shown above. Often the opening date is given incorrectly as 1837, which was the year of the death of King William IV. Look again at the date shown in this picture and you will see that the middle eight is incomplete; this symbol meant half of eight. Therefore we have the date 1848. *(LJ)*

Adelaide's arms. This sounds like an inn name rather than the 'marital arms of William IV and Queen Adelaide as used by her with her cypher AR' (defined by Windsor Herald, College of Arms). The other arms on this building is the royal arms as used during her husband's reign. In the early 1980s there was a building plan for twenty-three car spaces and various flats and houses with the proposal to demolish these listed buildings. Local people objected to the loss of these Hampton Court-style almshouses and they won the battle. *(RC)*

Pictured are some of the 1840s almshouses in Belvedere Road. The area seems to have been popular for almshouses at this time. *The Times* of 26 June 1841 reported on the Fellowship Porters' Chapel and Almshouses, where: 'Notwithstanding the very rainy state of the weather . . . yesterday morning his Royal Highness Prince Albert . . . arrived to the spot at 12 o'clock . . . exact to his appointment'. He was to lay the first stone helped by 'children of the Norwood School of Industry', who sang a hymn, and 'the Honourable Artillery Company playing "Rule Britannia"'. *(RP)*

This is the corner of Church Road and Belvedere Road, with the Alma very prominently to the left. The stone-laying ceremony probably occurred here as there was an intention to build a chapel in the complex and this is the central spot. Alderman Lucas took a leading part at the 1841 ceremony here, and was also prominent in the Watermen's Almshouses ceremony of 1840. He was concerned with fund-raising for both organisations. He had been Lord Mayor of London and must have used this prestige to the advantage of charitable causes.

These shops are the same type of building as the more obvious ex-almshouses in Belvedere Road. It seems that funds ran out, so all the houses were rented out or sold and the chapel never built. *The Times* reported that the weather became favourable for the ceremony and 'the regulation of the police prevented accidents . . . but one of the nurses . . . had stationed herself on a lofty platform used for gymnastic exercise, fell from her elevation and was . . . hurt'. Human nature does not change. Thanks are due to John Coulter who provided *The Times* report.

A little girl stands at the corner of Albert Road and Parish Lane, *c.* 1910. The postal area is now SE20. 'The Metropolitan Association for Improving the Dwellings of the Industrial Classes' built these cottages in Beckenham in 1866–8. The movement for better houses had been championed by Prince Albert, as shown by his model dwellings built at the Hyde Park Crystal Palace. Interest in better housing for the less well-off gathered pace in the mid-nineteenth century and the Alexandra Estate was at the forefront of this development. Rents were kept low but all expenses were paid from these and a tiny profit made. A superintendent made sure rules were maintained, such as 'no washing outside on a Sunday'. In about 1960 the houses were sold to the sitting tenants or others willing to buy. The estate is now a conservation area. *(NTC)*

This is Plas-y-Green, a cottage which stood in Penge when it was very rural. In the eighteenth century 'Penge Green' is recorded on maps for this area and the cottage was probably built at that time. It was demolished in about 1890. The reason for the Welsh name and who gave it is unknown. Possibly it was named with some humour, for 'plas' means palace or mansion; so it is a 'Palace in (the) Green'. It was in Kent House Road near the railway, on the Penge side of the road, and was also called the Welsh Cottage. *(LJ)*

5

Sweeping Changes

This is the still existing 1790 York House. Dr Kay Shuttleworth, a pioneer of public education and particularly the training of teachers, researched in the 1830s and '40s at the Industrial School which stood where Westow Hill meets Church Road, near where the Crystal Palace was to be built. He founded Battersea Training College in 1840 at York House, one of the first establishments of its kind in England. Some scholars from the Norwood Industrial School were among the first students. Eventually the principle of universal elementary education was established by the Act of 1870. A School Board was set up to ensure that all children had a school place. It took some years to achieve this, as the cost to parents was 1*d* or 2*d* a week, according to the number of children they had at school. Church schools, like St John's, Penge, often charged higher amounts.

Two boy chimney-sweeps were sent from Beckenham at 4 a.m. to clean a chimney in Dulwich. On this snowy morning, as they approached Penge Common, one collapsed into a snowdrift. He was barefoot and eight years of age. He asked his companion, aged ten years, 'Jack, get help from home'. When Jack returned with help, his little poorly clad companion was dead. This incident is reported by Thomas Campbell, the poet, who lived at Sydenham from 1804 to 1820. In 1808 a boy of Beckenham parish was apprenticed to learn 'the trade mystery and art of a Chimney Sweeper'. The master was not to force an apprentice to go up any chimney when it was 'actually . . . on fire', and to treat the apprentice 'with as much humanity and care as the . . . employment will . . . admit of'. This, then, was frequently the lot of poor, often orphaned, children. It avoided the support by the parish of some proportion of the poor. Many parishes used 'apprenticeships' in this way at this time. This chapter refers to improvements that avoided this kind of tragedy.

The 1834 Poor Law Amendment Act changed how the poor were to be treated. They were to be treated harshly; the attitude seemed to be that the poor were responsible for their own poverty. Larger units were encouraged so that a number of parishes could more economically cater for the poor. Penge in Surrey joined nine Surrey parishes to form the Croydon Poor Law Union. The large buildings built for the poor by these new units of local administration were called 'Union' Workhouses. The sites of modern hospitals are often those of the old workhouses, usually nineteenth-century constructions, which normally had infirmaries as part of the complex. Examples are Bromley, at Farnborough, Lewisham Hospital and Mayday Hospital at Croydon. Kindly registrars often recorded on birth certificates only the address of a workhouse when a baby was born there, thus avoided the condemning word 'workhouse'. In the case of Croydon, for example, this was 76 Eridge Road, with no mention that this was the workhouse address. The workhouses were eventually included within the remit of the Local Government Board set up by the government in 1871. The new board advised local Guardians to treat inmates more kindly. Dickens's novels had, to some extent, helped to change attitudes.

There were also changes in law and order. Bow Street Horse Patrols, set up in 1805, patrolled the district mainly from Croydon and Rushey Green in Lewisham. The Metropolitan Police was formed in 1829 by Robert Peel. In May 1830 some of our area, including Penge, was brought within the Metropolitan Police jurisdiction. Police houses, later called police stations, were built at Gipsy Hill in 1858 and Penge in 1872. The Gipsy Hill police station originally stood near the top of Gipsy Hill. The building used today is on Central Hill.

In 1840 the penny post was introduced by Rowland Hill. The sending of communications changed from the preserve of those who could afford the old, slow and expensive system to a cheap, fast and efficient service. Within London, in the late nineteenth and early twentieth centuries, you could virtually guarantee delivery in six hours. A reply to a letter could then be made and delivered on the same day. Telephone services started in the late nineteenth century but were not really a national or an efficient service until about the First World War. Telecommunications after this time were increasingly used for speedier communications.

Alexandra School, *c. 1950*. The records of this school, on the Beckenham and Penge border, show that if the children did not present the money they were normally sent home and the endorsement 'He did not return' frequently appears. By an Act of 1891 education in School Board elementary schools was made free. It was only in the late nineteenth century that compulsion was possible and all eligible children attended a school. *(GJ)*

Education developed for all in society in the nineteenth century. Churches, early in the century, were pioneers in providing some education for the poor. The National Society was Anglican and the British and Foreign Society was favoured by Nonconformists. The Bromley Road School, Beckenham, was founded in 1818 as a National School and there were 'British' schools at Sydenham and Norwood. The government in 1833 granted £20,000 to be shared between these two societies. After this there was a slow increase in government interest and funds for education. Before 1833, in England, the policy of governments was to keep out of education.

The Parish Vestry was the early form of local government. They did not always meet in the church vestry but often in such places as inns. Through the nineteenth century various authorities and 'boards' were set to govern aspects of society. Penge had many changes of local government. Until 1855 the Vestry of Battersea was, on paper, responsible for Penge. In fact for most purposes, Poor Law and road repairs for instance, Penge operated independently from 1838.

The nineteenth century witnessed the change from undemocratic control of local affairs to something like the system we have today. Voting rights were given to more groups of people. Borders and names have changed, but by 1900 we can see our

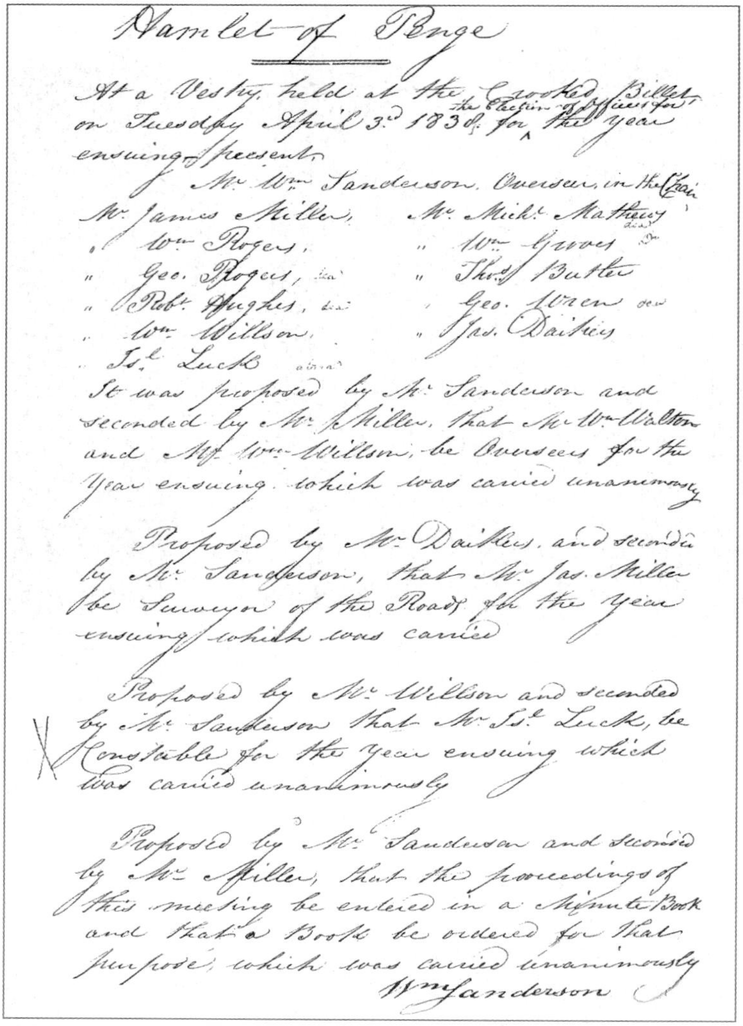
Hamlet of Penge

At a Vestry held at the Crooked Billet on Tuesday April 3rd 1838 for the Election of Officers for the year ensuing present

Mr Wm Sanderson, Overseer, in the Chair
Mr James Miller, Mr Michl Matthews
" Wm Rogers, " Wm Groves
" Geo. Rogers, " Thos Butler
" Robt Hughes, " Geo. Wren
" Wm Willson, " Jas. Daikies
" Isl Luck

It was proposed by Mr Sanderson and seconded by Mr J Miller, that Mr Wm Walton and Mr Wm Willson be Overseers for the Year ensuing which was carried unanimously

Proposed by Mr Daikies, and seconded by Mr Sanderson, that Mr Jas. Miller be Surveyor of the Roads for the Year ensuing which was carried

Proposed by Mr Willson and seconded by Mr Sanderson that Mr Isl Luck, be Constable for the Year ensuing which was carried unanimously

Proposed by Mr Sanderson and seconded by Mr Miller, that the proceedings of this meeting be entered in a Minute Book and that a Book be ordered for that purpose which was carried unanimously

Wm Sanderson

Penge operated as an independent Vestry from 3 April 1838, as this minute shows. This is the first page of its first known minutes. The railway is fourteen months from opening and Mr William Sanderson is the chairman of the Vestry.
Mr Sanderson had earlier bought the common land where the Croydon Railway company wished to build their railway. He allowed this on condition that a station was built there. When asked what name it should have he is reputed to have said 'My house is the only house', which sounded like 'Anerley howse' in his Scottish accent. Thus we have 'Anerley', which is recorded as Scottish English for single or alone. It is known that his house was called Anerley House, Hamlet of Penge, in 1841 and that it was known as Anerley Lodge in 1871. The station was called Anerley Bridge and later just Anerley. Places such as Anerley Gardens and the postal district of Anerley are therefore derived from this solitary house on Penge Common. Mr Sanderson's house does not exist today. *(BPL)*

present system of local government emerging. The London County Council and other such councils were established by Acts of 1888 and 1889.

In 1855, under the Metropolis Management Act, Penge became part of Lewisham. The first report on drainage by a Lewisham official reported that sewage from the Crystal Palace flowed in open ditches adjacent to houses. Penge was in urgent need of good drainage if disease was to be avoided. In 1857 Penge was included in south-east London for postal purposes, as were parts of Beckenham. Beckenham Urban District Council existed from 1894 to 1935 when it became a Borough Council within Kent.

The London Government Act of 1899 allowed Penge to change its status and become an Urban District Council in Kent by the end of 1900. So Penge was administratively in Kent for just over 65 years from 1900 to March 1965. Penge, like Beckenham, became part of the London Borough of Bromley in 1965. Some developments in the Crystal Palace area and its services and organisations follow.

My thanks to Mr Barry Reid who sent this picture from Australia and is descended from the Reid family shown here. This is the first known appearance in this country of a picture of Anerley House which eventually gave its name to the whole of the postal area of London SE20. Even Penge Town Hall is now called Anerley. William Sanderson (c. 1800–71), centre, was partnered in his silk manufacturing business by James Reid, the gentleman wearing the top hat. The house dates from about 1835 and was sold with its grounds in 1877.

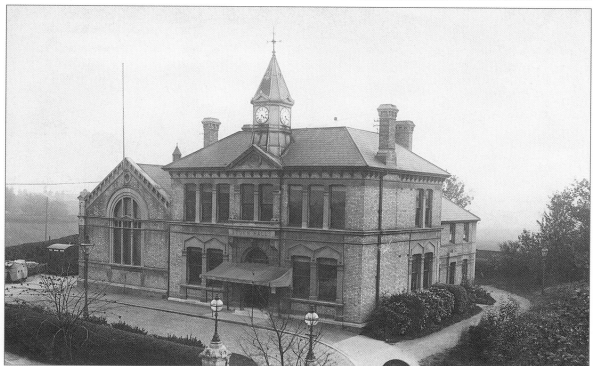

Penge Vestry Hall. This smart building, with illuminated clock, was built in 1878 on ground purchased, after much haggling, from the North Surrey District Schools. The picture was taken in about 1910 and is described as 'The Town Hall, Anerley'. The Penge Vestry Hall was built in Anerley Road near Anerley station. When the station first stood here it was said in *Kelly's Directory* for 1859 that 'there is no place by that name'. For the whole time the Vestry held meetings here, other administrations did much of the executive work. Penge sent representatives to other councils or boards such as Lewisham Board of Works and later the London County Council.

Town Hall, Penge, *c.* 1925. In 1900 the Vestry became Penge Urban District Council (PUDC). The first meeting of the PUDC was in November 1900 and gradually the new council took on wider responsibility until they had to extend the building. This extension doubled the frontage of the office building and it opened in July 1911. The Court Room extension foundation stone shows that it was built in 1923 behind the building seen here. It is now mainly Anerley Library. The town hall was for the whole of the PUDC area which included Anerley and part of Norwood (SE19). Correctly it was Penge Town Hall, situated in an area called Anerley by the postal authorities. There never was a council for Anerley and yet the board outside states 'Anerley Town Hall'. Effectively, this is its name now.

Croydon Union. This monogram above the Oakfield Road clinic has 'Relief Station', its old function, written across the C for Croydon and U for Union. From 1836 to 1930 Penge was in the Croydon Poor Law Union. This was the 'station' from which those in financial distress received money or 'outdoor relief', which was a far better fate than being admitted to the workhouse which gave minimal comfort and was intended to bring shame on the inmates. Under the Poor Law Amendment Act of 1834 small parish workhouses were eventually closed and Unions of several parishes formed into one administration. In north-west Surrey there were nine parishes stretching from Merton across to Penge and down to Coulsdon.

These initials mean London School Board and can be found on many old London schools; Haseltine Road School, Sydenham, and others have such indications of their origin. Interestingly, Penge was under Greenwich district, which included Lewisham, from the 1870s to 1902. This small stone is all that is left of Oakfield Road School, a typical London School Board school.

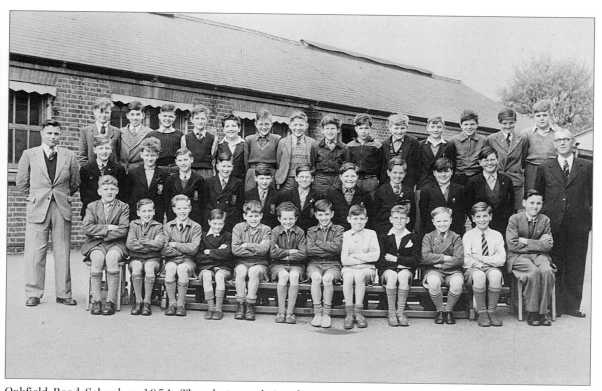

Oakfield Road School, c. 1954. The photograph is taken against the backdrop of the woodwork shop and metalwork classrooms. The school backed on to the main railway with four tracks. The noise was greater in the steam age. The teaching was interrupted every time a train passed, the teacher making no attempt to speak above the noise in some of the worst-affected rooms. The men are thought to be the headmaster, Mr Margham, on the right and a teacher, Mr Jenkins.

Hawthorn Grove. This road had a mixture of houses which were swept away for the post-Second World War 'improvements'. The happy community spirit can be glimpsed in this 1937 coronation picture. The change, for some, to flats in high-rise buildings was not liked and people began to detest living in this environment. Now most of the Groves towers have gone and this road is mainly lined with houses. At the end of the Grove the outline of Oakfield Road School can be seen in the picture. *(LJ)*

St John's School, *c.* 1890. The Church of England school was situated diagonally across the road from Penge police station. The building stood there from 1837 to 1937. It started as a chapel with Sunday schools. When St John's Church was built in 1849, the building was converted into St John's School. To begin with it took all children from about five to eleven years of age.

St John's School with an electricity-driven tram on the right and pedestrians bustling about their business, *c.* 1910. By this time it was St John's Boys' School. It had a high standard and reputation, drawing pupils from a wide area beyond Penge. Boys often got City office jobs when they left this school. Exceptionally by 1910 some pupils stayed on after the age of fourteen. Nationally the school leaving age was raised to twelve in 1899 and fourteen in 1918. Secondary state education, for a minority, started in the first decade of the twentieth century. *(NTC)*

St Paul's, Penge's second C of E school, was built in about 1870 in Hadlow Place. Conditions were very cramped, for it catered for up to 250 pupils of all ages in just one large hall, two small rooms and no playground. While an Education Committee of 1906 found it 'in good order', by 1924 the premises were said to be 'unsuitable for continued recognition', and infants travelled to Oakfield Road School owing to lack of space. It closed after the summer holidays in 1930 in a major reorganisation of Penge schools, when pupils moved to a new Anerley Junior School behind the Town Hall. The school building also functioned as the hall for St Paul's Church. In April 1971 the old St Paul's Church was closed and until a new church was built, the building became St Paul's Church Centre, as seen here. The building in which generations had gathered for school, youth organisations or church social gatherings had a short life after this as Penge Christian Fellowship's centre, and when they moved elsewhere it was demolished. *(CD)*

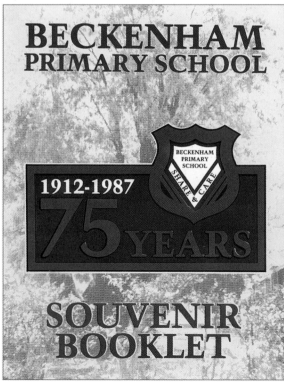

Anerley School, 1959. Anerley Junior and Infants School was a fine 1930s brick construction. It was demolished under a 1960s' reorganisation. The children all appear happy in this infants' class. The class teacher is Mrs Brenda Porteous. A subsequent school of steel and plastic has, in the twenty-first century, pupils from homes where sixteen languages other than English are spoken as the first tongue. *(CP)*

Beckenham Primary School. The names of our local suburbs are found in many English-speaking countries. On the outskirts of Perth, Western Australia, there is a Beckenham which is full of roads named after places in the southern London suburbs. The author spoke on local history to the top classes at the Australian school, and had to field difficult questions like 'Which Beckenham would you prefer to live in?' At all events the school's welcome left a good impression and the children lived up to their motto 'Share and Care', as shown on the souvenir booklet illustrated.

Rural-looking Beckenham police station, *c.* 1880. On 30 September 1835 *The Times* reported that 'The village of Beckenham . . . has been infested by a most lawless set of fellows who sometimes plunder the farmers . . . a horse and chaise from the churchwarden. . . . They have . . . taken up residence' here 'in consequence of the arrangements respecting the new police . . . acting at Norwood, Penge-common and Lewisham on the other side'. So they had been 'driven' to a 'peaceful village'. Eventually, after long years of requests, Beckenham got its police station. In 1884 the police station was moved to the new police building on Church Hill. *(LJ)*

Fire services. The object standing in the front of the island is a street fire alarm. Before telephones were commonplace these 'break the glass and pull the handle' alarms were seen every few hundred yards. This one would ring a bell in the fire station which was next door to the 1880 Beckenham police station. The picture above shows the fire station on the extreme left. This old building is still there at the corner of Burnhill Road and Beckenham High Street. Stone Farm, Park Langley, is in the centre of this view. Stone Park Avenue starts from here today. The lamps are Japanese-style, as is the garage built here much later. It is now known as the Chinese Garage. The Japanese style was introduced by the owner of Langley Farm, later Langley Court, who had spent some years in Japan. *(BL)*

Old house, 1902. In 1880 this building stood opposite the police and fire stations and was demolished in the early twentieth century. The house is typical of a medieval yeoman's house which originally had one fireplace in the centre of the ground floor, with no chimney. The smoke would vent through a hole in the roof. At one or both ends there would have been private rooms for the yeoman and his family. The house pre-dated the 'ER 1547' accession of Edward VI, shown on the wall. The other date, 1902, was for the coronation of Edward VII. W.H. Smith's shop now stands on the site. *(BL)*

The oldest working police station in the Metropolitan area is shown here. This is Penge police station at the junction of the High Street and Green Lane, *c.* 1900. From 1830 Dulwich, Penge, Sydenham and Norwood had been within London's police control. At first the nearest police houses or stations were at Camberwell Green or Brixton Washway. The Penge Vestry, in 1869, requested the Metropolitan Police to provide a station. A temporary station was set up on 2 May 1870 in what is today Penge High Street, near where the post office stands. This permanent station on the opposite side of the High Street, then described as 175 Beckenham Road, opened on 17 May 1872. *(NTC)*

Journalists reported a Beckenham crime as a Penge crime in 1877. In fact poor Harriet Staunton arrived at Forbes Road, Beckenham, late at night and was dead in less than 18 hours. This part of Beckenham by 1877 was Penge, for postal purposes. Mrs Staunton had, the evidence suggests, been starved to death at Cudham over months and brought to Forbes Road to die. This 1900 picture, from the Penge end near Montrave Road, shows the type of middle-class house that Harriet was nursed in for less than a day. The only involvement of Penge was that a person in Penge post office reported suspicious circumstances, and enquiries were then made about registration of the death, which had to be completed in Beckenham. *(NTC)*

The part of Forbes Road where Mrs Staunton died was just over the border from Penge, in Beckenham parish. The inquest was held at the Park Tavern in Beckenham, seen here, which was opposite the end of Forbes Road – or Mosslea Road as it is now. After the inquest and trial doubt was thrown on the decision by various people including '700 physicians and surgeons'. Those found guilty had their sentences reduced. Even though the papers called it the 'Penge Murder' the stigma aspect seems to have been exaggerated. Both Beckenham and Penge continued to attract many people of all classes. Penge had already seen the development of most of its building land and had by 1877 overtaken Beckenham in total population.

The Royal College for the Blind started at 42 Anerley Hill, seen here, on 1 March 1872. 'The neighbourhood had been carefully chosen; the Crystal Palace was then the musical centre of England, and the founders intended that their ambitious plans for the musical education of their pupils should derive every possible advantage from that fact. . .' (from *The Royal Normal College for the Blind, A Short History*, by Dr J.N. Langdon BSc, PhD). The college was founded by the first Duke of Westminster, Mr C.A. Miner, Dr T.R. Armitage and Sir Francis Campbell, the first principal. The last two men were blind. More accommodation had soon to be found on this site and later in Westow Street, because the number of pupils increased rapidly. In the early twentieth century 44 Anerley Hill was the local suffragettes' office. *(RCB)*

The long-term premises of the Normal College for the Blind were gradually built near Westow Street, Upper Norwood, seen here. The hills were utilised for physical exercise and adaptations were made for all sorts of sports including cycling. A swimming pool was built and many blind children were taught to swim. In September 1940 the college moved to Shropshire because of the war. The college in Norwood received bomb damage and there was no happy return. The Royal National College for the Blind moved several times and is now situated in College Road, Hereford. The word 'Normal' in the original title was used in the same sense as in France at the time, to indicate teacher training. They had a greater number of these students when in London than they have at Hereford today. *(RCB)*

North Surrey District School building and pupils. Here the girls were instructed mainly for domestic service and the boys often joined the Army or Navy. In this picture from about 1890 a drummer and band can be seen to the left. Often the musically gifted boys would climb to officer rank to lead some of the best regimental bands. In 1851 there were 464 inhabitants at the school including 44 staff and their families. Over 700 children were eventually in residence and they had 55 acres of playing fields and farmland. *(NTC)*

A school swimming pool had been added to the already extensive sports facilities by 1900. No one here is afraid of the master of a workhouse and if they asked for more food it looks as though they got it. The children were from the Croydon Union and many others, including Lewisham and Wandsworth. When the school opened in November 1850 the Archbishop of Canterbury and the Bishops of London and Winchester attended. Charles Dickens was also invited to visit.

Workhouse children in a production of *HMS Pinafore*, *c.* 1905. By this time the school was humane even by the standards of today. Several clerics over the years had positions of responsibility there and influenced the banning of corporal punishment though this was virtually general practice. The children were to be well dressed so that they were indistinguishable within the community. It seems certain that many of the scholars were better fed than the poorer children living in the south London suburbs, so that locally, in an inverse fashion, they could be distinguished. *(NTC)*

Anerley Girls' School was a private school, one of many existing all round the Crystal Palace in the late nineteenth and early twentieth centuries. The school, near North Surrey District School and also in Anerley Road, did not survive the war. The 1934 picture shows one teacher to every ten pupils. The children often progressed to the 'County' schools. The boy in the back row is Yves Jaulmes, just eleven years old, whose parents were French. In 1939 he was called up from Genoa Road, Anerley, where he lived with his parents, into the French army. Eventually after capture by Rommel's men in North Africa, he was released by the German Army in France. With his future wife he helped Allied airmen escape from Paris to Spain. He is now widowed and lives in Beckenham. He and his wife tended to play down the dangerous activity they undertook under the noses of the Nazi forces. *(YJ)*

Anerley Girls' School, 1928. It is typical of the large houses of the late nineteenth century which were favoured by moneyed families. A comfortable home with a large garden could be enjoyed by the city gentleman and his family. Travel to London was easy and quick by train from Anerley station. Neighbouring houses in 1900 were occupied by Oppenheim Broad and Henry Klein – an indication of how the Crystal Palace helped to draw people from far and wide. German families were plentiful all around the Crystal Palace, evidenced by the German Church in Sydenham. Upper middle-class families abandoned such houses from 1900 to 1939, and they became schools or businesses, and later were sometimes converted to old people's care-homes or flats. This house at 206 Anerley Road is now twelve flats.

Pupils at St Christopher's Preparatory School, 1936. There were about 100 pupils at this private purpose-built school in Lennard Road, Beckenham, built in about 1930 and bombed on 29 December 1940. Hazel Burgess was the only person killed. She was the eleven-year-old niece of the head, Miss Carlton, on a short Christmas holiday visit. The school was not rebuilt. Jean McDonald, now Mrs Ruthen, is thanked for this photograph. She is in the back row of girls, second from the left.

This was part of the Alexandra Cottages estate, built 1866–8. It has always been called 'The School' and there is evidence that it was used as such for a brief time and for adult lectures on subjects such as science in the 1870s. The occupants of the 164 Alexandra Cottages in 1871 had a total of 64 trades. The buildings are now divided into homes. In 1875 a tailor living there spoke in favour of a new Board School to be built for the 280 children living in the cottages. The reporter at the meeting wrote that the tailor 'was almost pathetic when he spoke . . . of the want of that education which had been denied him in his youth, but the blessings of which he was anxious to secure for his children'.

The high churchman of St George's, the Revd William Cator, was reported as saying in 1875 that Board Schools were for 'gutter children'. Seemingly he wanted to delay the provision of adequate school places so that the high church could influence education in their schools when these were eventually built. Fortunately other views prevailed and the Board became responsible for the expansion of Alexandra School in Parish Lane, SE20. The new Beckenham School Board of 1876 aimed to provide a place for every child. Alexandra had mixed infants', girls' and boys' schools on this site. In 1900, the time of this picture, the Senior Boys' headmaster lived in the house on the right. Corporal punishment was often harsh up to the 1950s. *(NTC)*

These boys are the Alexandra Junior School team that won the 'Crystal Palace and District Cricket League' in 1934. Corporal punishment was infrequent in this school. Mr Broadbent is the games master on the left and Mr Dent, the headmaster, is on the right. Back row, left to right: Sparks, Vickers, Ben, Bone, Tassel, Minter. Front row: Hammond, Copper, Wellard, Townsend, Emblen, Baker. At least two of these lads were killed in the Second World War. Mr Bernard Copper is thanked for this picture. *(BC)*

Penge County School for Boys. This building when opened in January 1931 was correctly called the Beckenham and Penge County School for Boys. Because it was located in Penge, school inspectors often omitted the word 'Beckenham'. The boys were previously at the building marked 'Technical Institute' which still stands near Beckenham Library. Beckenham Council was early in providing secondary education for a small minority of fee-paying pupils in 1901. The County School boys' use of these playing fields was envied by the majority of boys who attended such schools as Alexandra and Oakfield Road Schools. These older 'Senior Elementary' schools only had small asphalt playgrounds. Today the buildings to the left are Royston Primary School and to the right the Bromley Adult Education College, Kentwood Centre.

The Beckenham and Penge County School for Boys Junior Chemistry Laboratory, 1931. The 'County' schools were so called following Balfour's Education Act of 1902 when counties became responsible for them. In 1907 schools such as this had to offer at least 25 per cent free places. The competition to gain a 'scholarship' or free place was intense. The vast majority of children were left with an elementary education with very little chance of progress in subjects such as chemistry. If a child's parents were able and willing they would pay fees at the 'County', where there were normally places available. Fees for county and state subsidised schools were abolished in 1944 and secondary education slowly improved for all.

Dulwich College, 1903. Bowler-hatted groundsmen are at work in front of the 1857 college designed by Charles Barry Junior. The college is within a mile of Crystal Palace Park and in 1903 the Palace building dominated the scene from the college grounds. There were very many who could afford the day fees locally. Others sent their children here to board from far and wide. One American here was Raymond Chandler who created the character Philip Marlowe. 'Marlowe' was possibly chosen since a house of the school has this name. The list of the famous who attended the school is long. Another literary figure is the inimitable P.G. Wodehouse.

This type of tricycle was pedalled around Beckenham as a private subscription library service until Beckenham Borough Council opened their first library in 1939. Mr Henry Cox of 115 Victor Road made a living out of his fellow rate-payers with the books on his delivery tricycle. There were also Smith's, Thornton's and Boot's subscription libraries in Beckenham High Street. This municipal action contrasts with that of Penge, which used the rates to provide reading facilities in the nineteenth century – giving them a 40-year lead on Beckenham's library services.

Penge Public Library, *c.* 1900. This pair of houses at the corner of Laurel Grove and Oakfield Road formed the first permanent library in Penge, opened in 1899. The building no longer exists. In 1892 reading rooms were opened at the corner of Anerley Station Road and Minden Road; that building is still there. In 1928 Penge Library moved to Oak Lawn at 194 Anerley Road and in 1946 was the first municipal library to lend out gramophone records. There was for many years an active Gramophone Society based at the library. The library was large and had a good reputation. In the 1960s this building had to be demolished. *(NTC)*

The nearest large medical institution to the Crystal Palace is St Christopher's Hospice in Lawrie Park Road, on the border of the Beckenham old parish and Sydenham. Dame Cicely Saunders was its founder in 1967. This lady enlightened the medical world and opened the door to the whole hospice movement. She wanted attitudes changed towards the dying. The hospice has 62 residential beds and a variable number of outpatients, normally around 80. The emphasis is on life and care, with relief of pain, right up to the end. There is a chapel within the building and the Christian faith is the inspiration for the work. There is a constant stream of nurses and doctors attending postgraduate training there.

6

Total War & Peace

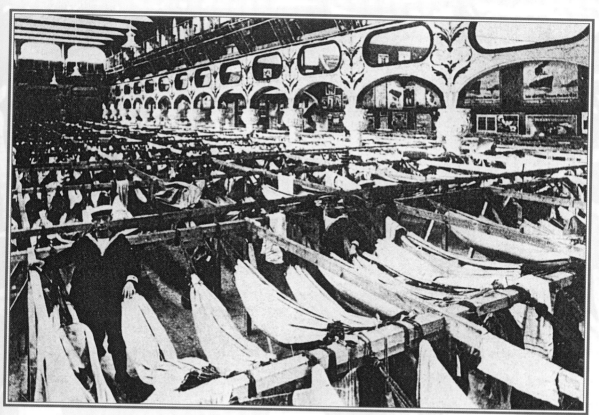

Even within the space provided inside the Crystal Palace the men are cramped in their
sleeping accommodation. The hammocks on the frames are slung about every 18in.
Influenza spread rapidly at the depot in 1918 and there were over a hundred fatalities.
The depot was closed for two weeks to try to control the spread of the disease. *(EP)*

There can be little doubt that war in the twentieth century reached home. With the 1903 invention of heavier than air powered flight man was quick to turn this to a weapon of war. Thus in the two world wars the enemy was not only at the door but in many cases blasting through the roof. Men also still marched off to the front, full of optimism and hopes. Problems would be solved. We still struggle in the twenty-first century with idealism propounded as our reason for defence, or attack. More unsettling is the lack of knowledge of our enemy. Who is he, and how and when will he strike?

As an example, the Beckenham deaths from enemy action show more civilians killed than servicemen in the Second World War. Included in these figures is 'friendly fire' which killed at least 5 per cent of people locally. Another trend is unmanned remote killing. Locally, during the retaliation weapons era of the last ten months of the war, V1 flying-bombs and V2 rockets killed about the same number as manned 'conventional' weapons in the first five years. No wonder many people were nervous of remote-controlled weapons during the cold war years.

During the war, Baird organised weapon production in the grounds of the Crystal Palace. Muirhead, Small Electric Motors, and many other factories were on war work and important railway lines criss-crossed each other locally. The London County

Penge was part of Battersea in recorded history for over 1,000 years and this Celtic shield is called the Battersea Shield, having been found in the Thames there. Dating from 350–50 BC, it is on display at the British Museum. It is thought that the shield was a flamboyant display item and not lost in battle. It is likely that it was used as a votive offering. It is made of sheet bronze 'with twenty-seven framed studs of red enamel'. It shows the craftsmanship of our Celtic forebears who named Penge and therefore lived somewhere nearby. Julius Caesar must have seen such shields even if not at the time when he is reputed to have crossed the Thames at Battersea.

This is the Penge railway bridge which carried visitors to the Crystal Palace in 1854. The shelter of this bridge was used for religious services by Catherine Marsh, her brother-in-law, the Revd Mr Chalmers, and others from St George's Church, Beckenham. Their congregation, in hundreds, was the men engaged on creating the Crystal Palace and grounds. A works corps was being formed in 1855 to be a part of the Army in the Crimea. Catherine Marsh was greatly respected by many of the men joining the Army Works Corps for they worked, or had worked, at the Crystal Palace. She gave them practical help like offering to look after whatever portion of their pay they wished to save in a Friendly Club she organised, using the Savings Bank. Miss Marsh also wrote short wills if a man indicated this was needed for his dependants. About this time a boxing match turned into a fight with the police and Catherine stopped this before there were any fatalities. Her words were, 'The first man that throws a stone is my enemy . . . by God's help'. The so-called Battle of Penge ended.

Council area was evacuated in September 1939. These were the much publicised and comparatively fortunate children. It was a strange and eerie experience for the author in September 1939 to find no children in Sydenham, which was about 700 yards from his home on the Beckenham/Penge border. Some children were killed in the unevacuated, officially designated 'neutral' areas of Kent such as Penge and Beckenham. Hindsight must blame the deaths on this policy. Fairchilds' school very near Biggin Hill RAF station and other schools adjacent were likewise left to their fate.

Whereas 'official' evacuees were assisted financially, the privately evacuated had to pay all their costs, even following the bombing of their homes. Those with uninhabitable houses had to live in shelters until they organised their own relocation, normally to a safer part of the country. Teachers, Citizens Advice Bureau staff and many other kindly volunteers did their best to help. Places like Penge and north-west Beckenham were eventually evacuated in January 1941. Many in any case had already gone from these areas before this official action. When the bombing decreased, most people returned to the area and the authorities were quicker in 1944, during the flying bomb and rocket attacks, to officially evacuate the whole local area.

Peace returned in 1945 only to be followed by many smaller wars in which local people died. Moreover in 1993 an IRA bomb exploded, by chance, next to Alexandra Infants' School.

Colonel Bourne DCM, OBE, known as Colour Sergeant Bourne of Rorke's Drift – the battle of 22 January 1879 featured in the film *Zulu*. Frank Bourne was only twenty-five at the time, although he was depicted by actor Nigel Greene as older in the film. He was not awarded the VC from this action. He eventually reached a higher rank than Lieutenants Chard and Bromhead who were in command at Rorke's Drift. Bourne retired from the Army in 1907, only to serve again in the First World War. He retired again in 1918 with the rank of honorary lieutenant colonel. He lived at 16 King's Hall Road, Beckenham, for two decades of his retirement. He died on 9 May 1945, probably the oldest survivor of Rorke's Drift. Both he and his wife are buried at what was the Crystal Palace and District Cemetery (now the Beckenham Crematorium and Cemetery).

In the centre is Prince Dabulamanzi kaMpande who led the attack on Rorke's Drift. He was half-brother to King Cetswayo of the Zulu Nation. The Zulus shocked the British Army at Isandhlwana where they defeated Lord Chelmsford's forces who suffered the loss of 1,700 men. This was a surprise attack and some retreating survivors warned the British at Rorke's Drift, who had time to prepare for an attack. The Zulu were unable, with overwhelming numbers, to defeat the 150 defenders of Rorke's Drift on the night of 22/3 January 1879. In July 1879 the British decisive victory at the Zulu capital, Ulundi, ended the Zulu War. This war and the Boer Wars, 1880–1 and 1899–1902, had shown that a 'modern' army could suffer defeat. It is now thought by many that these wars were the beginning of the decline of the British Empire.

Private Herbert Baker Edwards lived in Penge and was distinctive in that he served in the Indian Army in 1910, as seen here, and later in both the world wars. Between these activities he married and had two children as well as qualifying as a dentist, setting up a practice in Samos Road, Anerley. Here he is with his pith helmet, a sun-hat issued to the army in India, at the ready. Maggie Hantken, née Edwards, is thanked for this photo. *(MH)*

Private Edwards, like many other local lads, is in this picture of the 5th Battalion the Royal West Kent Regiment at camp at Crowborough, Sussex. He eventually falsified his age in order to serve in the Second World War. One wonders how many of these boys survived the cold trenches, which they were shortly to experience, following this happy relaxed scene. *(MH)*

Whit weekend 1918 was notable for a bombing raid by Gotha aircraft. On the night of Sunday 18/19 May bombs were dropped in Sydenham; Leeson's Hill, Chislehurst; Queensmead and Beckenham Lane, Bromley. There was damage to property and in Sydenham 18 people were killed and 24 wounded. Of the dead five were servicemen, billeted, the author was informed, in the new shops where the shattered window caused terrible injury and death. The shops were opposite the corner of Fairlawn Park shown here. This site in Sydenham Road was rebuilt. The grocery shop C. Ware in the picture was replaced by another called Burgess, and Collingwood's butcher's shop was built on the opposite corner. An unlucky spot, for both corners of Fairlawn Park, shown here, were bombed in the Second World War. *(LL)*

Civilians are recorded on a First World War memorial inside All Saints' Church, Trewsbury Road, Sydenham. The twelve people named at the base of the memorial were killed on 19 May 1918, on the corner of Fairlawn Park and Sydenham Road, by the bombing of a German Gotha twin-engined airplane. These planes were fast and replaced the Zeppelin in raids on London from the end of 1917. Zeppelins had also flown over the Crystal Palace area and made good targets for the new British fighter pilot heroes.

From 1915 until 1918 the Admiralty used the Crystal Palace for training in several disciplines including signalling, as illustrated. The steps featured are one of the few features of the old Crystal Palace still existing in the twenty-first century. The title 'HMS *Crystal Palace*' was colloquial and used by both servicemen and locals. The semaphore message is 'Royal Naval Division', an official title. *(EP)*

Some of the 10,000 men did go overboard with their drinking in the neighbourhood of the Crystal Palace. Organised recreational facilities were a salutary vent for their energies and the YMCA did their bit in helping these men. The one civilian is probably Mr Hodgson of the Penge YMCA. This chess club seems to be taken very seriously by the sailors, who presumably had to wear their headgear even when they were relaxing inside the Egyptian Court. *(BPL)*

Bombardier Willson is posed loading a shell with his guncrew in 1918. The British Empire lost a million men killed in the First World War. In August 1914 it started with the optimistic popular belief that it would 'all be over by Christmas', and that it was 'the war to end all wars'. Its very title 'First' is now indicative of that forlorn hope. The few months turned into over four years of a very harsh fighting existence for the soldiers, often in the mud of the trenches with heavy slaughter. *(CD)*

1918
Oct 30th Cambrai
Nov 1st Morencourt
- 2nd Vendecies
8th Jenlain
- 9th Bry
- 11th Feignies
Armistice signed
Returned to La Louche
Nov 29th 1918
On Leave Jan 15th 1919

Depart for Osthgin in
Germany March 25th 1919
Arr 29th =
Went to Oberstieg
- - - Eil
- - - Engelskirchen.
Eil

On Leave July 1919
Back to Eil
From Eil to Kehl
left Battery Oct 16th 1919
Demobbed at Crystal Palace
Oct 22nd 1919

The end came as a surprise to even the French and British commanders who had planned attacks for dates beyond the Armistice of 11 November 1918. The diary of Lance Bombardier Willson, who lived in Alexandra Cottages (see pp. 82 and 100), shows in a personal way the story of the decisive final advance. The last entry 'Demobbed at the Crystal Palace' must have come with great relief for Mr Willson. Thousands of others must have associated the Crystal Palace with this happy end of war service. *(CD)*

This is the captain of the ABC 1913–17,
M.W. Calder, who was killed in action at Vimy
Ridge, on 3 May 1917, while serving in the
Honourable Artillery Company. The ABC, or
Anerley Bicycle Club, started in 1881 when
two types of machine were in use; the
ordinary, 'penny-farthing' high wheeled
bicycle and the tricycle. Both had solid tyres
and both were used in championship races.
The 1881 riders had to master greater skills
than was demanded by the later safety cycle.
However, cycling became very popular in the
1890s when pneumatic tyres were more
common. The club's present secretary is
thanked for her help, as is the archivist
Mr N. Greig.

Many Germans attracted by the Crystal
Palace set up their homes in its vicinity.
Some worked locally and set up businesses,
others had often diplomatic jobs in central
London. At the end of the nineteenth
century Britain had close ties with
Germany and people, at that time, on both
sides were friendly towards each other. The
German Evangelical church shown here
was built in 1883 in Dacres Road, London
SE 23, for the large numbers of Germans in
the vicinity of Forest Hill and Sydenham. It
suffered damage in the Blitz, and from a V1
flying bomb and a V2 rocket. *(LL)*

This German Lutheran church, by G.S. Agar, opened in 1959 and replaced the bombed church described on p. 113. The church is named after Dietrich Bonhoeffer (1906–45), who was pastor of the old church from 1933 to 1935. Even in the mid-1930s he struggled against the Nazi regime. He was part of the German resistance and was arrested in 1943, sent to Buchenwald concentration camp and hanged in 1945. He had been involved with the anti-Hitler conspirators who made an attempt on Hitler's life. The present-day church incorporates a study centre and archive to perpetuate the memory of the Germans who worked in the anti-Nazi resistance movement. *(LL)*

Virtually every hamlet and town in Britain has a memorial in a prominent place, normally dating from just after the First World War. The Revd Canon Smyly of St John's, Penge, dedicated this memorial on 25 September 1921 to 'those connected with the Hamlet who gave their lives for King and Country'. John A. Carleton of the Salvation Army read a passage from scripture with a 'proud ring of conviction in his voice . . . enhanced by the memory of his son and grandson who met their death in the Irish Sea through the ruthless enemy submarine'. The quotes are from the *Penge and Anerley News* of 1 October 1921.

The Penge memorial has 412 names from the First World War but none for the Second. There is a dedication to servicemen and civilians 1939–45, but with no details. Individual organisations often dedicated their own memorials such as the Maple Road Baptist Scouts' memorial shown here (left).

The Watermen's Company memorial reads 'In memory of the Freemen and Apprentices . . . this Asylum was restored in 1920 by the subscriptions of members and friends'. The word 'asylum' was still used in 1920 whereas today almshouses is normally used. This practical memorial in Penge is an example of the many halls, hospitals and other buildings which featured as memorials.

The Revd Philip Venables, Vicar of St John's, conducted the Remembrance Service on 9 November 2003. This wreath is placed by a member of the 101 Cadet Detachment, the Princess of Wales Royal Regiment. About 250 people were present compared with 6,000 at the dedication of this memorial in 1921. After the 2003 service local councillors and others enjoyed warm drinks, courtesy of St John's Church helpers.

Sea Cadets of the Training Ship *Sikh*, Beckenham and Penge unit, marched from their HQ in Kent House Road to this Remembrance Service, 9 November 2003. Scouts with their flag have also arrived early and are on the left of the picture. This Beckenham memorial displays the names of about 700 servicemen killed in 1914–18 and 300 in 1939–45. There are 330 civilians, including 30 Civil Defence personnel and 12 firemen. The author knew some of these civilians ranging from John Hawkes, aged four, to George Dominy, retired from the Royal Navy, aged eighty-one.

The Revd Ernest Barson ejected William Joyce from Penge Parliament which allowed all shades from communists to right-wing speakers in their debates at Kenilworth Hall, Penge Congregational church. Just before the Second World War 'The Speaker', Mr Barson, conducting the meeting, decided that Joyce should be thrown out. Joyce lived at 41 Farquhar Road, London SE19, in 1933–4. He fled to Germany just before war broke out and made propaganda broadcasts for the Nazis from September 1939 to April 1945. He used a pretentious upper-class accent and was dubbed 'Lord Haw-Haw' in Britain. He made all sorts of threats against Britain, even mentioning local places such as Penge. Perhaps he felt offended. He was executed as a traitor after the war. A road in Penge, near St John's Church, is named after Mr Barson, a tireless worker for the district. He was Minister of Penge Congregational church 1909–47 except for a break in the First World War, when he was a YMCA Padre, as in this 1918 picture.

This air-raid siren struck terror into many a mother's heart when it screamed up and down to warn of approaching enemy bombers. It stood on Penge police station from 1939 until the 1980s and now only the platform remains. The All-Clear was a welcome continuous sound. At lunchtime on 20 January 1943 the siren gave no warning. Low-level fast fighter-bombers had evaded British detection. The author and many other schoolchildren ran for cover as shells or machine gun bullets impacted all around the Penge/Beckenham border, where there were no casualties. Sandhurst Road School in Catford was bombed, and thirty-eight children and six teachers were killed. The news unusually was not suppressed since its propaganda value was recognised.

Named after John Anderson, the Home Secretary 1939–40, the Anderson air-raid shelter was made of corrugated iron. The shelter on the left of the picture saved the lives of three of the Smith family at 2 Tennyson Road on the night of 19/20 September 1940. Frederick Smith, the father, was outside in the garden and James, his son, was in the house. Both were killed. Alexandra Hall Mission building is the ruined church-like building in the centre. Over twenty houses were damaged including the author's parents' house. Since Beckenham was 'neutral', but nobody had told the enemy this, my parents had to pay for evacuation in order to find somewhere to live.

Friday, September 20th. 11-10 a.m. First warning of the day. I saw a number of planes go over making towards Thames + the guns were firing at them. I heard one bomb dropping. All clear at noon. I went out this morning + found that bombs dropped last night in Parish Lane — several roads leading off. Alexandra Mission (Methodist) is ruined. It was this that woke me at 2 a.m. when I heard the crashes + the sound of breaking glass.
7-30 p.m. Warning. Just as I was going out 'shelter-visiting'. Guns as usual started at once. Did not hear early morning all clear.

Saturday, September 21st. 11-10 a.m. Warning. Lasted only 20 min.
6-10 p.m. Warning. All clear in an hour. We saw our fighters going over a good deal. At one time 12 of them came low over the house making towards Croydon.
8-10 p.m. Warning. The usual barrage broke out a few minutes after as the noise of Raiders was heard.

Sunday, September 22nd. 2-30 p.m. First warning of the day. I was at Dr. Clark's + left at once for home. A German bomber passed over fairly low but the clouds hid it. Went to church at 3-45 for Baptisms. While service was in progress the All Clear came — 4-10 p.m.
4-45 p.m. Another warning as we were having tea. All Clear at 6-8 p.m. Just in time for Church!
7-10 p.m. Warning five minutes after people came out of church. ... his the usual nightly raid ... after midnight we home ... ... I heard the All Clear at other warning at 3-30 a.m.

... Warning lasting just over 'this morning' ... us going five minutes before ... at the Shaws (Langton Grove.)

... were having tea. Chislehurst 20 of our fighters going over after 6 p.m. while the King ...ease

ENEMY LOSSES

COMPARATIVE FIGURES

FROM OUR AERONAUTICAL CORRESPONDENT

Up to yesterday morning a total of 2,241 German aircraft had been shot down over and around the British Isles. The R.A.F. had lost 568 aircraft, from which 271 pilots were saved.
The respective losses this month are as follows:—

	German	British	R.A.F. Pilots Safe
Sept. 1	25	15	9
,, 2	55	20	9
,, 3	25	15	8
,, 4	54	17	12
,, 5	39	20	9
,, 6	46	19	12
,, 7	103	22	9
,, 8	11	3	1
,, 9	52	13	6
,, 10	—	—	—
,, 11	89	24	—
,, 12	3	—	—
,, 13	2	—	—
,, 14	18	6	—
,, 15	185	25	13
,, 16	7	—	—
,, 17	12	3	—
,, 18	48	12	9
,, 19	5	—	—
	781	217	112

The Revd Bernard P. Mohan was vicar of St John's from 1936 to 1946. During the Second World War he rode out on his bicycle, with a helper, virtually every morning, 'shelter-visiting' around his Penge parish. He comforted those who had lost loved ones and did what he could, actively seeking those in need. Only by his diary entry for 20 September 1940 do we know that the Tennyson Road incident was at 2 a.m. The Beckenham Alexandra Hall Mission he refers to was non-denominational. Thanks are due to the Imperial War Museum. *(IWM)*

Raids came mainly at night from September in the 1940–1 Blitz. There were day raids but the heaviest bombing was during the hours of darkness. It was normal to retreat every night into whatever shelter was available. Some went to public shelters, often within school grounds. Chislehurst Caves were a safe haven for thousands. The author vividly remembers the cold and damp of the family Anderson shelter in the back garden, with a small oil lamp to illuminate a game of Ludo or cards. This picture was probably taken very early on 10 October 1940. Three of the Reardon family are recorded in the Beckenham records as killed on 9 October, at their home, 13 Marlow Road, SE20. *(BPL)*

This large modern Co-operative store was bombed on the evening of 6 November 1940. Three people were killed, two seriously and two slightly injured. Clothes, furniture, household appliances, gardening equipment and many other items including food of all sorts could be bought. The store was rebuilt in the same style after the war and flourished until the 1970s. It has now gone the way of most such stores. In 2004 Sainsburys have a mainly food store on the same site, next to the Moon and Stars, Penge High Street.

These buildings and those beyond the railway bridge were destroyed by flying bombs. The whole area including the left side of the picture was destroyed or damaged beyond repair in July 1944. Before the bombing 241 Beckenham Road was the Midland Bank, shown here on the corner of Mackenzie Road. David Greig, grocer, is in the centre of the picture at nos 233 and 235. The author witnessed the start of the VI attacks when, in June 1944, a pair of flying bombs passed directly over this site. It appears that this was a flight path to central London. False information was fed to the enemy through an English double agent, Mr E. Chapman, who was really only working for Britain, indicating that these missiles were landing north of central London. They were convinced by this and shortened the range. The result was very heavy bombing all around the Crystal Palace, some miles south of the flats and office blocks of central London.

Beckenham Road in about 1910 shows a scene which ended at lunchtime on 2 August 1944, when a V1 destroyed all but the first house on the right. The bomb killed 44 people. Most people were at lunch, and 27 were killed at no. 199, Mrs Richards' dining rooms, which was on the left of the picture. This was the highest number of fatalities during the war for an incident in the present Borough of Bromley. This flying bomb was one of a pair, the other landing harmlessly in Hayes. (Figures from Lewis Blake, *Red Alert*.)

This 1944 photograph shows a helmeted lookout on the Churchfields Road Small Electric Motors (SEM) works. A detailed record survives of their frequent warnings to staff to take cover. Whether a warning was on or off, the firm provided their own alarm system and had to keep details of every minute lost through warnings. This was completed night and day throughout the war so that lost time was detailed for official records.

The HMS *Belfast* compass casing, called a binnacle, was made by SEM, as were numerous electric motors, for a variety of functions. Other SEM-manufactured parts to be seen on this ship include the switching gear made in the Laurel Grove Works, Penge. The captain's chair, on the bridge, is in the foreground of the picture. HMS *Belfast* is moored on the Thames in the centre of London and forms part of the Imperial War Museum.

The cruiser *Belfast* is one of the few Second World War fighting vessels left in the world. She took part in the sinking of the *Scharnhorst* off northern Norway on 26 December 1943, the D-Day landings and the Korean War. In 1939–45, 'savings weeks' were held to raise an amount equivalent to the cost of a warship, or other military hardware.

The band passes the saluting platform outside the Empire, Penge, for War Weapons Week. Those on the platform probably include Councillor Frank Smith, honorary secretary of the Savings Committee, and Colonel Chambers. The aim was to raise £50,000, and £90,000 was the successful result in the week of 19–26 April 1941.

This is the entrance to Alexandra Infants' School, Beckenham, in 1989, where the headmistress, Mrs Day, supported by her husband, has just concluded a golden anniversary celebration. Many former pupils were invited to the place which first introduced them to education. In retrospect early education in the 1930s was a carefree and sunny part of the author's pre-war life. Fortunately, we children thought that there was real 'peace on earth and goodwill towards men'.

This happy peaceful Alexandra Infants' School was to be threatened on 3 February 1993. A warning had been given by the IRA that two bombs were on the 9.05 a.m. train from Victoria to Ramsgate. Prompt action by the authorities brought the train to a halt on the line immediately adjacent to the school at Kent House station. Indeed the platform was not long enough and the rear coaches projected over the play area of this and Royston Primary School. These rear connecting carriages had to be evacuated by three brave policemen who boarded the train and supervised the passengers, who were still unaware of the danger. There were twelve carriages and the explosion was at 9.50 a.m. in the seventh carriage, very near Alexandra Infants' School. The police had done their job of evacuation well. There were no casualties.

7

People & Pleasure

A charabanc drawn by four horses is providing a day out for Small Electric Motors staff, *c.* 1914. Most have Edwardian-style best suits and all have a hat. This could have been Derby Day when many firms organised a visit. Pleasure seems to be taken very seriously. *(SEM)*

The hilly land 6 or so miles south of Westminster and the City of London has long provided diversions. The heights, in the nineteenth century, had on their higher ridge the Crystal Palace, its pleasures attracting millions. Earlier, the 1066 charter mentions the grant of hunting in Penceat given by William I to the Abbot of Westminster. This is written evidence of the area's long association with recreation. The spas or wells at Norwood, Dulwich and Sydenham attracted people from the fashionable areas in and around the City of London. Samuel Pepys mentions that his wife would have her fortune told by a gipsy in Norwood in the seventeenth century. The gipsies were a distinctive people of the area until the Vagrancy Act of 1797 and the early nineteenth-century enclosures of Croydon, Lambeth, Lewisham and Penge commons. The gipsies enjoyed the relative inaccessibility of the area and are recorded by the road Gipsy Hill and railway station, of the same name. The gipsies seem to have been accepted in the community, as shown by the prestige enjoyed by Margaret Finch, the queen of the tribe. She had a house near today's Gipsy Hill and, at a reputed 109 years of age, was buried in St George's churchyard, Beckenham. Many gipsies married out, eventually to leave descendants here today.

The first public picture gallery in England was built in Dulwich in 1811–14. In 1829 William Hone and his artist friend Samuel Williams attempted to visit the gallery, but it was closed. Instead they took a walk from Dulwich through a 'cathedral of bird song', which was the present Crystal Palace Hill and grounds.

Near Clock House, in Beckenham, the road to Penge crossed this bridge with a ford on both sides. The drawing was made by Samuel Williams as he accompanied William Hone, the writer, on a ramble from Dulwich in May 1829. They had a beautiful rural walk crossing the Croydon Canal at a bridge in Penge. The Chaffinch river no doubt attracted songbirds and this is where birds were trapped for city dwellers by professional catchers. *(BPL)*

Dr Glennie's academy at Dulwich, 1820. Lord Byron (1788–1824) was a pupil for two years before continuing his education at Eton and Cambridge. Here he wandered in what he describes as: 'Spring green lanes,/With all the dazzling field-flowers in their prime,/And gardens haunted by the nightingale's/Long trills and gushing ecstasies of song.' Perhaps because he met such people as gipsies locally it had an influence on his life, since he always championed the oppressed. He managed to mitigate a bill in Parliament which, if he had not intervened, would have prescribed the death penalty for the Luddite smashing of machinery. He helped the Italian revolutionaries and died of disease in 1824 while training the Greeks, who were fighting for their freedom from the Turks. His wife, Lady Byron, stayed in Beckenham with her daughter.

They then dined at the Crooked Billet, Penge, on 'eggs and bacon, and spinach put in the pot from the garden . . . and we had the pleasure of . . . a comfortable parlour with a bow window view of the common . . . The House affords' services as good as 'any retired spot so near London'.

The two friends then continued over the Chaffinch river, into Beckenham and along 'a nearly straight road' to West Wickham. The quotes are from *The World of William Hone* by John Wardroper. Here we have a written record of our area traversed in the nineteenth century.

We know that later in the nineteenth century personalities and great writers, such as Charles Dickens, John Ruskin, H.G. Wells and Sir Arthur Conan Doyle had an interest in the area. Charles Dickens's fictional character, Mr Pickwick, retired to Dulwich; which has a Pickwick Road in its centre. John Ruskin lived at Herne Hill and voiced his opinion strongly against the Crystal Palace. H.G. Wells lived as a boy in Bromley and is said to have cycled and played around the Crystal Palace. Conan Doyle lived in Tennison Road, South Norwood; one of his books was *The Norwood Builder*. A few great people and some local people, virtually unknown outside small communities, are recorded in the rest of this chapter.

A mile to the south-east of Dulwich Wells was the popular Sydenham Wells, sometimes known as Lewisham Wells and even Dulwich Wells. This is the Green Dragon, as sketched by Thomas Bonner in about 1770. It was one of about a dozen wells that attracted Londoners in the period 1640–1830. George III visited for one day, with Life Guards to protect him. The waters were said to cure many diseases including scrofula; some even claimed it was a cure-all. Visitors would make a round day trip from London on a holiday; the better-off invalids and pleasure seekers would stay longer, and this stimulated building in this area. The Green Dragon stood opposite where Taylor Lane meets Wells Park Road today, but the inn was destroyed by a V1.

Wells Park, c. 1900. This beautiful recreational green area today evokes the scenery that originally attracted people to this spa. The St George's Bowmen used one of the well's houses as a headquarters from which they had wide open areas for archery practice. This beauty and use of open space was ended or compromised by the enclosure of the common. During the Second World War a local story has it that an enemy airman bailed out of a damaged bomber and landed in the park. He was very fortunate for he was treated well, residents giving him a cup of tea for shock. Other accounts are similar in that bombed people were ready to be vengeful but only met another mother's son. Some injured men recognisably cried out for their mothers.

Betty Saville has collected her share of brushwood from Penge Common in 1825. The painting is by W.P. Rogers and he calls it *Study from Nature*. At this time the common is still a resource for ordinary people and no doubt attractive, as described by William Hone. In a few years the common will be enclosed. Poor Betty will possibly be cold and short of fuel for cooking.

The Maple Tree, Penge. This is not a photograph of the pub but one of a painting by Ron Woolley, an artist, who has exhibited at the Royal Academy in London. Ron travelled widely after study at Beckenham Art School. He was born in Penge and partly educated at what he jovially describes as 'Oakfield Road Academy', in other words Oakfield Road Elementary School. He retired and returned to the SE20 area where he can enjoy a pint at the Moon and Stars with old friends. For the first 100 years of its existence the Maple Tree was the The Crown. The frontage was only up to and including the third window on the first floor. Beyond that was Young's stationers.

This is the 1947 Beckenham Business Houses' Annual Beauty Competition. The organisation also covered firms beyond Beckenham. The house in the background was formerly Langley Court near the Chinese Garage, in 1947 the offices of the Wellcome Beckenham Laboratories. The young lady on the left of the picture is Miss SEM and next to her is Miss Twinlock. On the right of the picture is Miss Kohnstamm representing a large leather processing factory which then operated near the railway bridge where Long Lane meets Croydon Road, Beckenham. *(SEM)*

Rogers' Store, Penge, and a jolly annual day out for the staff in the early 1920s. It is clear that this was a really big highlight in the year. The ladies are in their finery which they probably bought from the store. Hard rubber tyres on the charabanc indicate that this was before the general use of pneumatic tyres. Dunlop patented pneumatic tyres in 1888 for cycles and they were first used on racing bicycles in 1889.

Rogers' old premises serves many purposes in the twenty-first century and one part is now a mosque. The mosque is situated near the old Rogers' cashier's office where money was received and change despatched on overhead wires. The system is explained on p. 130.

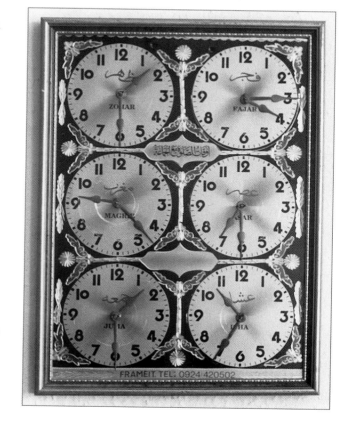

These clocks show prayer times, which change throughout the Islamic year and in accordance with the geographical location of the mosque. The clocks are periodically adjusted by the Mullah. Prayers are said six times daily either here in the former shop, or where it is practicable.

Rogers' store, and the world of yesterday's 'Are you being served?'. Young assistants in the haberdashery department are Edna Ely on the left and Beryl Corner, who is thanked for this photograph of 1946. Here the customer could get dozens of shades of ribbons. To the right of the picture is a chair that gave young legs a rest while mother spent what seemed an eternity making her choices. At the end was the excitement of the cash transaction which involved the machine above the assistants' heads being used to send money shooting along a wire, in a small container near the ceiling, to the cashier.

The Lamson Rapid Cash Carrier, single wire with spring propulsion, would bring your one farthing back if you insisted on your change rather than pins. The same systems are to be seen in the Cabinet Rooms in Whitehall. Rogers, described as a draper in 1936, sold lengths of cloth for the housewife to make clothes, curtains or bedding. Up to about 1950 everything seemed to be sold with 11¾d at the end of the price. There were 960 farthings to a pound sterling and a packet of pins was proffered, rather than give the one farthing change. Barlow World Vacuum Technology, of Gosport, are thanked for the use of their illustration and help given.

This is the largest store in Penge, truly a Co-operative department store, 1939. Across the High Street was Bryce Grant's which provided a wide variety of goods as a 'general drapers'. Edgintons' furniture shop now occupies much of the former Bryce Grant space. There were also a number of waitress-service restaurants. Such were conditions in the 1930s that Miss Spicer, headmistress of Alexandra Infants' school, could close the school at lunch-time and dine at the pleasant Bryce Grant restaurant. There were four large shops not 100 yards from Penge police station, Rogers, Bryce Grant, the Co-op and Olby. These did not last to the end of the twentieth century.

Avril Sydnee is thanked for allowing me to quote parts of her poem, 'Penge':

> Penge was an exciting place, when I was very small
> We went to buy our fruit and veg from a market stall . . .
> And then to shop at Rogers for me was most appealing
> There was this funny whizzing thing that raced across the ceiling.
> You gave it all your money, it really was quite strange
> Because it whizzed right back again, and in it was your change!
> Elastic, lace and ribbons, you bought them by the yard
> Coloured plastic buttons, in sets sewn on a card . . .
> Assistants prim and proper, with condescending smiles
> Guarded glass-topped counters on each side of the aisles.
>
> There was a shop called Olby's with toilet bowls on view
> Baths and taps and basins, all shining white and new
> 'Oh to have a bathroom', my mother often cried.
> We shared one with Aunty Rose, and our toilet was outside!
> The Co-op was a mystery, to which I was not privy.
> They gave you little metal coins to save up for your 'divi'.

Mr Thomas Crapper (1836–1910) was born in Yorkshire, lived in Thornsett Road, SE20, and was buried in Crystal Palace (now Beckenham) Cemetery. Olby's shop in Penge proudly displayed sanitaryware in the 1950s and '60s when this was acceptable. When Crapper displayed his new sanitarywares at his Chelsea showrooms in the 1860s, it is said that ladies observing the bowls became faint at the shocking sight. It was Crapper who popularised and patented certain improvements for cisterns in flush toilets. He fitted his wares in famous places like Sandringham, Buckingham Palace and Westminster Abbey. Thanks are due to Simon Kirby of Thomas Crapper and Co. Ltd for the use of the photograph and advice.

Also buried in Crystal Palace cemetery, near Thomas Crapper, is Frederick York Wolseley, who gave his name to the Wolseley motor car. He died at 20 Belvedere Road, Upper Norwood, in 1899. It was one of his cars that was chosen for this 2002 wedding. Wolseley is credited with producing Britain's first 'horseless carriage' in 1895.

Another Crystal Palace Cemetery local notable is the first really great cricketer, W.G. Grace (1848–1915). He had his home ground at the Crystal Palace from 1899 to 1908 when he was the secretary and manager of the London County Cricket Club. Dr Grace did practise medicine but his great interest was sport. He captained the English Test team against Australia in 1880 and 1882, and toured in Canada and the USA. (LJ)

After gaining the world record for the mile, with a time of 4 minutes 6.4 seconds, Sydney Wooderson is chaired by his fellow Blackheath Harriers (BH). This was at Motspur Park in 1937, without the help of the special synthetically surfaced faster tracks used today. Wooderson lived in Village Way, Beckenham, when younger. He ran for BH against Beckenham and Penge County School for Boys in their sports field at Penge. In 1946 in Oslo he beat the future Olympic Gold medallist Emil Zatopek and others to win the European 5,000 metres title. He now lives in Dorset and still takes an interest in the same club, which in 2002 was reconstituted Blackheath & Bromley Harriers AC. Thanks are due to Blackheath & Bromley Harriers AC for the photograph.

This firm started when Raffaello Tomei immigrated from Valdottavo, 12 miles from Lucca, Italy, in the nineteenth century. He and his uncle made and sold religious statues in south-east London, and this was expanded to include plaster decorations, such as cornices and ceiling roses. In 1875 a permanent workshop near Penge East station was established. The firm now has its offices and workshop at 42 St John's Road, about 200 yards from where the first workshop stood. Two sons of the original migrant were killed in the British Army in the First World War. Today the directors are Phillip and Paul, great-grandsons of Raffaello Tomei.

LEST WE FORGET

THIS TABLET IS ERECTED TO THE MEMORY OF
THE FOLLOWING EMPLOYEES OF THIS COMPANY
WHO FELL IN THE SECOND WORLD WAR

1939 – 1945

L. LOOKER	D. CART	J. CANNON	W. CANNON
H. CARTER	M. CORKERY	L. GARDNER	F. GLASS
L. GRAVES	S. HORLOCK	A. JENNINGS	K. JONES
G. MATTHEWS	J. NEWTON	W. RICKARD	C. RICKETTS
A. ROBINS	B. SKANE	D. TERRY	F. WHEELER

R. FITZGERALD – KOREA – 1952

PHILIP JOHN GARDNER
VC MC
1914 – 2003

WHO WOULD TRUE VALOUR SEE
LET HIM COME HITHER

From the corner of Versailles and Anerley roads, *c.* 1910. Local holders of the VC include Lieutenant Richard Jones of Thicket Road, Anerley, who won the highest military award, the Victoria Cross, for valour during a battle in which he was killed at Vimy Ridge in May 1916. He had been a pupil at Dulwich College and like many teenagers died fighting for his country. His parents lived in the first house on the right in Thicket Road, behind the hexagonal pillarbox, which dates from about 1870. The house is still there in 2004, but the letter box has been replaced with a later cylindrical model, a few yards up Versailles Road.

Another Penge VC who also died while winning this award was Private Herbert Columbine. He sent others away and continued firing his machine gun, although attacked from the air and facing overwhelming odds. His VC was won at Hervilly Wood, France, in March 1918. In the Second World War there were more local VCs including Captain Philip Gardner, of the firm by that name, who had already gained the MC.

The managing director of J. Gardner and Co. Ltd, after the Second World War, was Captain Philip Gardner VC, MC. Gardner, of the Royal Tank Regiment, who won his VC in an armoured battle at Tobruk in November 1941. He attempted to rescue a badly injured comrade under heavy enemy fire, was injured during the attempt and, disregarding his injuries, returned to make a successful rescue. Later he became a prisoner of war at Brunswick where he heard of the suffering of the people of London. He organised there a 'fund' of IOUs which he subsequently collected and used to start the Brunswick Boys' Club in Fulham, which survives in the twenty-first century. He was born in Sydenham on 25 December 1914, and attended Dulwich College. At seventeen he started work in the family business situated on the border of Sydenham and Beckenham.

The Howard family lived in Arpley Road and sold second-hand clothing there. Some of the Arpley people lived close to the stage door of the Penge Empire. The Howards, like their cry 'Rag and bones', will be remembered as part of the backdrop of living in the streets around SE20. In the 1930s and '40s Mr Howard senior was a familiar figure with his black Edwardian suit. Later the family had a shop in Southey Street, Penge. Mr Howard's daughter Millie worked from here and eventually traded from around the corner at 162 Parish Lane. The triangular shop on the corner of Bycroft Street had stalls outside loaded with a great variety of goods but especially clothes. The horse which pulled her goods round the area was stabled under the arches in Bycroft Street where her husband cut firewood for sale. Millie also wheeled a large pram for 'totting'. She was known as Millie Howard although she was Mrs O'Neill and had two sons. A grand old lady, and always cheerful, she died in 1998 at the age of ninety-two. The present-day descendants of the Howard clan, including Mrs M. Fowler, are thanked for the photograph and their help.

This 1920s scene shows possibly the grandest building locally other than the Crystal Palace – the Empire, Penge. Marie Lloyd featured in the opening show on 3 April 1915. Variety shows were followed by repertory. Plays intended for the West End were given a trial run in Penge. Circuses were a big attraction. Before any show free entertainment was given in the form of a parade of animals along the High Street. This gave many who could not afford entrance a wonderful view as the elephants, each holding the tail of the animal in front, walked majestically along. In 1949 the Empire became the Essoldo cinema; the building was demolished in 1960.

The Crystal Palace Band leads a parade along Anerley Park Road, c. 1930. Its name was the Upper Norwood Temperance Society Band from 1901 to 1924, and was changed in that year because of continuous engagements with the Crystal Palace Company. Under this name it competed with successes at regional and national levels, and is one of the few traditional bands in London to compete recently in the National Championships. The band raises money for St Christopher's Hospice, playing in schools and churches. The band's schedule, as this goes to press, includes playing on 5–6 June 2004 at the festival in Crystal Palace Park, 150 years after its grand opening. Thanks to Rachel Bleach, Crystal Palace Band Secretary, for the information and picture

The Spencer Royston Ballroom, 1980s. The true name of this building is 'Penge and District Trade Union & Social Club'. It is hidden away at the end of Royston Road SE20, and the ballroom is on the upper floor. The building is fondly and widely remembered since it housed what became known as the Royston Ballroom, where Peggy and Frank Spencer launched many successful Penge dancing teams. They won competitions such as the British Latin Formation competition in 1964 and three British titles in 1968. On a less ambitious level the Spencers' dancing school allowed couples to get acquainted and over 100 went on to wed, Peggy proudly announcing numbers week by week. All pupils had to be alcohol-free and smartly dressed when they entered. No alcohol was served in the ballroom. These rules were acceptable to late teenagers and people in their twenties in the years it operated here, 1950–75. People attended from a wide area and the Spencers made a big contribution to communal well-being. *(LJ)*

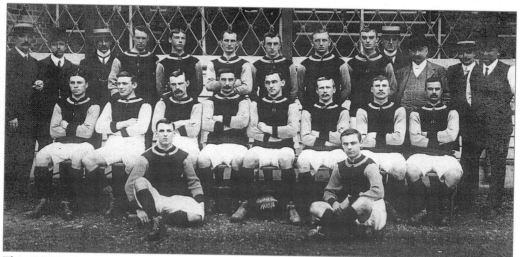

This 1905 photograph is the first one known of the Crystal Palace football team. Their managerial staff includes, top left, John Robson, the manager from Middlesbrough who recruited the players, mainly from the north of England. The brand new stand is featured behind the all professional team. In 1905 they were elected to the Southern League. They won the 2nd Division Championship of 1905/6 and in 1906 the team was promoted to the powerful 1st Division of the Southern League. The Crystal Palace Football Club had been formed from the workmen and officials at the Palace at least as early as 1871 and their unofficial name was the Glaziers. *(NS)*

The football ground, sometimes called the exhibition ground, here shows wartime neglect, August 1950. The stand mentioned on the previous page is in the centre. The FA Cup Final was played here from 1895 to 1914. In 1913 the gate was 121,919. The spectators were mostly standing on the banks but some had a vantage-point sitting in surrounding trees. The 1914 Cup Final was the first ever attended by the monarch. George V presented the cup to Burnley who beat Liverpool 1–0. The Crystal Palace Sports Centre athletic track is now on the site of the football ground and exciting world-class meetings give pleasure to millions when these meetings are televised. *(JB)*

Sir Ernest Shackleton (1874–1922), the Antarctic explorer, lived at 12 Westwood Hill as a boy. His father was a doctor here, next door to St Bartholomew's Church. Ernest attended a preparatory school, formerly situated on the southern corner of Jews Walk and Kirkdale, and then Dulwich College (1887–90), where he is a celebrated old boy. The Anglican church of St Bartholomew was built between 1827 and 1832. Workmen killed in an accident when the Crystal Palace was being constructed are buried here.

Admiral of the Blue Sir Piercy Brett was born in 1709.
He died in 1781 at the Clock House near where Beckenham Spa
stands today. He had sailed around the world with Anson in
the years 1740–4 when much treasure was taken from the
Spaniards. One of his exploits involved leading only fifty-
eight men to capture the town of Paita in Peru. They
took the treasure and burnt the town in 15 minutes.
In 1745 he was responsible for a possibly more
laudable naval action which helped to change the
course of history when he captained the *Lion*,
preventing Bonnie Prince Charlie's support ship, the
Elizabeth, from landing in Scotland. Captain Cook
(1729–79) was given his orders to survey New
Zealand and Australia and other places on his
voyage of 1768–71 by his superior Admiral Brett.
A cape near the Bay of Islands, New Zealand, was
named Cape Brett by Cook in honour of his
admiral.

The North Cloister of Dulwich College
houses the small boat *James Caird* in which
Shackleton sailed 800 miles from Elephant
Island to South Georgia. This difficult
navigation was accomplished in order to
organise the rescue of his remaining crew
left on the island. His ship the *Endeavour*
had been crushed in Antarctic ice and the
heroic story of the survival and leadership
of Shackleton and his men is inspiring.
Shackleton in his 1908–9 expedition
located the South Magnetic Pole and
reached a point 97 miles from the South
Pole, which was a record at the time. The
school has named a large block of
classrooms after him. The *James Caird* can
be viewed by the public after checking that
it is at the college. It is often loaned to
museums abroad, such is the interest.

Mr Graham-White left Crystal Palace in his Farman biplane on 15 June 1910 at 7.18 p.m. and arrived at Brooklands at 7.43 p.m. This caused a sensation at the time as most people had never seen an aeroplane. The balloon centre of Britain had been at the Crystal Palace and 1910 also marked the use of dirigibles at the Crystal Palace. The ascent of balloons from there had taken place since 1859, a gas pipe from the Crystal Palace Gas Works at Lower Sydenham being specially provided. Passengers were taken aloft and the British Association as well as Admiral FitzRoy were interested in using a balloon for meteorological purposes. The colourful ascent of balloons from the grounds of the Crystal Palace was spoken of by the author's parents. The flight of heavier than air machines was short-lived. Graham-White had to rig ropes across the landing strip, as used today on aircraft carriers, in order to stop safely. No flying fatalities were recorded here in 1910 even though they had an inadequate landing strip of less than 100 yards. One author has claimed that one of the Wright brothers flew an aircraft from the Crystal Palace grounds, but the Royal Aeronautical Society has no record of this.

The early British flying experiments with such organisations as the Aerial League of the British Empire resulted in the development of an aircraft-building industry in the United Kingdom. The zenith may have been our contribution to Concorde, for this aircraft was a demonstration of British and French skills, flying passengers at a speed greater than sound. This aircraft crossed the Crystal Palace Park, Dulwich, Norwood, Penge, Sydenham or Beckenham, according to the wind direction, almost daily. Concorde delighted our eyes for the last time on the afternoon of 24 October 2003. We were privileged to see the very last scheduled flight from New York. The Crystal Palace TV and telecommunications tower is claimed to be the tallest steel structure of its type in Britain. It was built in the former Penge Urban District in the 1950s and came into service on 28 March 1956. The tower was nearly 709ft in 1958 and later there were adjustments. Its owners, in 2004, give the height as 656ft. It stands on a hill 365ft high, making a total combined height of over 1,000ft. The tower is visible from most of London and beyond, so it could be regarded as a visible symbol of the functions of the Crystal Palace, providing pleasure to millions. *(DJ & CW)*

Her Majesty the Queen visits the Sports Centre to give encouragement at the London Youth Games held in July 2002. Here she is with some of the competitors. The Crystal Palace Sports Hall, seen here, is now a listed building. It is hoped by many that the sports complex will provide facilities for future Olympic Games.

ACKNOWLEDGEMENTS

I will not be able to thank the numerous people who have helped in this task and to whom I am most grateful. Chris Doran, Ralph Palfrey and Peter Canovan deserve individual thanks, as do members of the Bromley Local History Society, the Crystal Palace Foundation and Bromley Library staff, especially Simon Finch. Acknowledgements of help and thanks are due to the following: Dr Cavill of the English Place Name Society, Andy Currant of the British Museum Natural History Department, John Coulter of Lewisham Library, Mr Bennett of Croydon Library, Mr D. Deverall of Penge TU Social Club, Sue Breakell of the Imperial War Museum and local historian Cliff Watkins (CW).

I would also like to thank my close family, especially my daughter Helen.

PICTURE CREDITS

Conway Castle-Knight	CCK	British Museum (Natural History)	BMNH
Roger Cooper	RC	Imperial War Museum	IWM
Helen Johnson	HJ	Small Electric Motors	SEM
Leonard Johnson	LJ	Michael Long	ML
John Baber	JB	Bill Morton	BM
John Gent	JG	Patricia Knowlden	PK
Christopher Doran	CD	Neil Knowlden	NK
Jack Hilton	JH	Bromley Libraries	BPL
Chris Porteous	CP	Lewisham Library	LL
Brenda Porteous	BP	Croydon Library	CL
Eric Price	EP	Upper Norwood Library	UNL
Nancy Tonkin Collection	NTC	Revd Nigel Sands	NS
Glyn Jones	GJ	Mr Cohen	MC
Betty Lashmar	BL	London City Mission	LCM
Keith Burtonshaw	KB	Tim Martin	TM
George Brooker	GB	Les Hazelden	LH
Bill Brooker	BB	Ralph Palfrey	RP
Bernard Copper	BC	Royal College for the Blind	RCB
Infomart, Dallas	ID	John Warner	JW

Thanks are due to those listed above and the other people who loaned me pictures not used. Uncredited photographs are from the author's collection.

INDEX